A Chance to Make Good

AFRICAN AMERICANS
1900–1929

THE YOUNG OXFORD HISTORY OF
AFRICAN AMERICANS

Robin D. G. Kelley and Earl Lewis
General Editors

A Chance to Make Good

AFRICAN AMERICANS
1900-1929

James R. Grossman

Oxford University Press
New York • Oxford

For Ruth and Alice

Oxford University Press

Oxford   New York
Athens Auckland Bangkok Bogotá Bombay
Buenos Aires Calcutta Cape Town Dar es Salaam Delhi
Florence Hong Kong Istanbul Karachi
Kuala Lumpur Madras Madrid Melbourne
Mexico City Nairobi Paris Singapore
Taipei Tokyo Toronto
and associated companies in
Berlin   Ibadan

Published by Oxford University Press, Inc.,
198 Madison Avenue, New York, New York 10016

Oxford is a registered trademark of Oxford University Press

The poem on page 129, *If We Must Die* by Claude McKay, is reprinted by the permission
of the Literary Archives of Claude McKay, Carl Cowl, Administrator.

Grossman, James R.
A chance to make good: African Americans, 1900–1929 / by James R. Grossman.
p.   cm. — (The young Oxford history of African Americans: v. 7)
Includes bibliographical references and index.
ISBN 0-19-508770-4 (library ed.); ISBN 0-19-508502-7 (series, library ed.)
1. Afro-Americans—History—1877–1964—Juvenile literature.
2. United States—History—1901–1953—Juvenile literature.
[1. Afro-Americans—History—1877-1964.
2. United States—History—1901-1953.]
I. Title. II. Series.
E185.6.G88   1997
973'.0496073—dc20   96-8471
CIP

1 3 5 7 9 8 6 4 2

Printed in the United States of America
on acid-free paper

Design: Sandy Kaufman
Layout: Leonard Levitsky
Picture research: Lisa Kirchner, Martin Baldessari

On the cover: The Migration of the Negro Series, Number 3. *Jacob Lawrence, 1940-41*
Frontispiece: *Silent protest parade down New York City's Fifth Avenue, 1917*
Page 9: *Detail from* The Contribution of the Negro to Democracy in America *(1943) by Charles White, 11'9" x 17'3"*
Hampton University Museum, Hampton, Virginia

CONTENTS

ROBIN D. G. KELLEY
EARL LEWIS

INTRODUCTION

The years between the start of the twentieth century and the beginning of the Great Depression featured a mixture of promise and disappointment for African Americans. Only a generation and a half after the abolition of slavery, the rich hope for emancipation and freedom had given way to the harsh realities of Southern redemption, and, by 1900, the disfranchisement of black voters. As important, where once individual whites discriminated, with the turn of the century new structures and laws validated group discrimination and institutionalized second-class citizenship for blacks. So palpable was the change that the transitional years 1890–1910 have been referred to as the nadir in post–Civil War African-American life and history.

Currently we think of the first three decades of the twentieth century as the formative years of Jim Crow, or legal segregation. Yet in the face of discrimination and political neutering a new generation of African Americans nonetheless left an indelible mark on the nation and its affairs. Tuskegee Institute head Booker T. Washington and his many lieutenants assured blacks of patronage positions and other political favors in return for loyalty to the Republican party. Washington, in fact, counseled white politicians—from presidents to local officials. He and others showed the difference between not voting and having political clout.

Moreover, during this period blacks expanded the meaning of political. Some created and sustained a wide range of civic and protest organizations, including the National Negro Business League, the National Association for the Advancement of Colored People, the National Association

Marcus Garvey (in center, with sash), reviews members of his Universal Negro Improvement Association in a parade in New York City in 1924.

of Colored Women, the National Urban League, and the Universal Negro Improvement Association. At the same time intellectual activists such as W. E. B. Du Bois and Mary Church Terrell used the pen and the podium to agitate on behalf of civil rights. They joined an impressive roster of men and women who founded businesses, churches, educational institutions, and fraternal bodies to promote the building of black communities.

Of course average blacks did not leave their destiny in the hands of elites alone. Thousands voted with their feet, which may have been the most political of all acts. Between 1900 and 1920 approximately 1.5 million African Americans left the rural South, encouraged by recruiting efforts and the desire to leave the stifling racial climate in rural Southern communities, and aided by the nation's demand for labor during World War I. Scores settled in major urban centers in the Northeast and Midwest, among them New York's Harlem and Chicago's South Side. But they also moved to Detroit, Gary, Cleveland, Milwaukee, and St. Paul, as well as Philadelphia, Camden, Newark, and Boston. Often overlooked is the fact that the vast majority of the migrants moved to Southern cities such as New Orleans, Houston, Atlanta, Durham, Richmond, and Norfolk. In both the South and the North during this period, African Americans began the transformative process that would make them the nation's most urban residents by the 1960s.

This book explores the history of black life in the age of Jim Crow. It documents the efforts of individuals and communities to claim a place for themselves in America. It includes the voices and thoughts of blues songsters and Harlem Renaissance lyricists. It outlines the link between community development and racial consciousness. It is a book peopled by the ordinary and the famous, the migrant and those who stayed behind. It ultimately narrates the powerful story of black aspirations, frustration, and determination in the years bound by 1900 and 1929. It is the story of those who seized their chance to make good.

This book is part of an eleven-volume series that narrates African-American history from the 15th through the 20th centuries. Since the 1960s, a rapid explosion in research on black Americans has significantly modified previous understanding of that experience. Studies of slavery, African-American culture, social protest, families, and religion, for example, silenced those who had previously labeled black Americans insignificant historical actors. The new research followed a general upsurge of interest in the social and cultural experiences of the supposedly powerless men and women who did not control the visible reins of power. The result has been a careful and illuminating portrait of how ordinary people make history and serve as the architects of their own destinies.

This series explores many aspects of the lives of African Americans. It describes how black people shaped and changed the history of this nation. It also places the lives of African Americans in the context of the Americas as a whole. We start the story more than a century before the day in 1619 when 19 "negars" stepped off a slave ship in Jamestown, Virginia, and end with the relationship between West Indian immigrants and African Americans in large urban centers like New York in the late 20th century.

At the same time, the series addresses a number of interrelated questions: What was life like for the first Africans to land in the Americas? Were all Africans and African Americans enslaved? How did race shape slavery and how did slavery influence racism? The series also considers questions about male-female relationships, the forging of African-American communities, religious beliefs and practices, the experiences of the young, and the changing nature of social protest. The key events in American history are here, too, but viewed from the perspective of African Americans. The result is a fascinating and compelling story of nearly five centuries of African-American history.

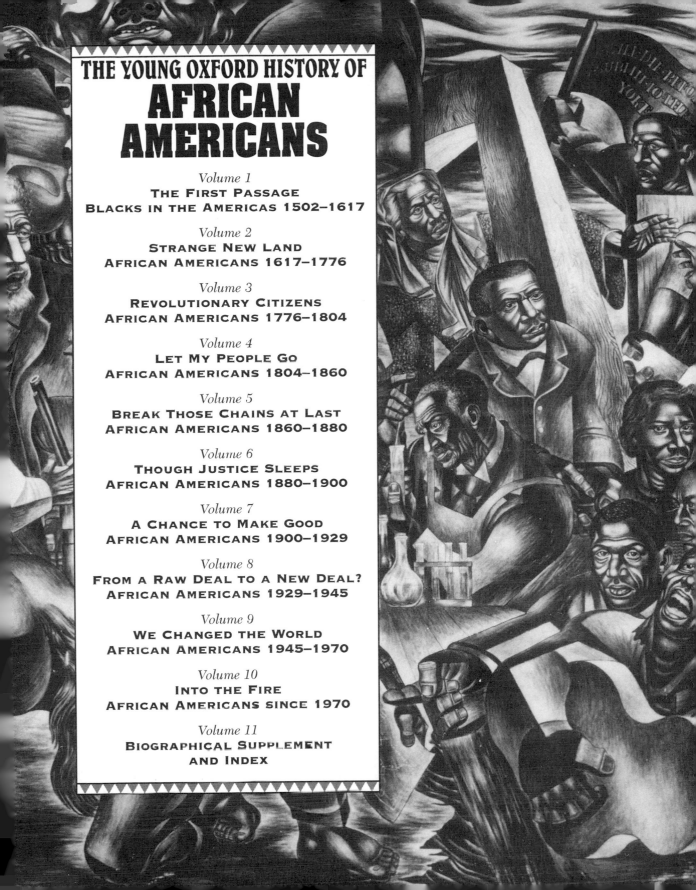

THE YOUNG OXFORD HISTORY OF
AFRICAN AMERICANS

PROLOGUE

M innie Savage knew farm work. Born in 1902 to sharecroppers in Ackenback County, Virginia, she entered the
fields barely seven years later. By the time she was 10,
her daily routine resembled that of thousands of other
African Americans across the rural South. She worked
from dawn to dusk, she later recalled, "plowing, cultivating, you name it."

School had to be squeezed in between the November harvest and
February planting. As the eldest of six children, she could contribute the
most to the family income and therefore toiled in the fields while her
younger siblings absorbed the little education that was available from the
poorly funded school for black children. A younger sister carried home
lessons for Minnie to work on at night, but the evening tutoring sessions
brought only limited results. After a day's labor under the hot sun, Minnie
was usually too exhausted to concentrate. Despite her parents' resolve to
secure an education for all their children, Minnie logged only five years of
schooling.

Minnie's grandparents had been slaves. By the time Minnie was born
they had experienced the exhilarating hopes of emancipation and Reconstruction and the disappointment of its collapse under the pressure of
white terrorism. Years later, after decades of life in the North, Minnie
recounted memories of her parents "still in bondage. What I call bondage
is that they was still livin' under some of the slave rules." These rules combined an oppressive *economic system* with a *code of behavior* that translated white supremacy into everyday life by defining subordinate roles for
black Southerners.

Black Virginians, like their peers elsewhere in the region, were
excluded from some public places. In others they were relegated to

*Women at work picking
cotton in a Louisiana
field about 1924.*

separate facilities, which always were poorly maintained and visibly inferior. Segregation was enshrined in law. Black Southerners also had to endure daily indignities such as being expected to step aside (out of the road if necessary) when approached by a white person.

By the time of Minnie's birth, the legislation defining this system was less than a generation old, although the customs upon which these laws were based had existed since the days of slavery. Minnie referred to both law and custom as "old arrangements" and later recalled how she and her friends talked about their unwillingness to endure such conditions.

Minnie at last saw the possibility of relief from farm work during her teenage years because her brothers were now old enough to take her place among the crops. She had always dreamed that she would stay in rural Virginia "and have a big house and six kids and be like the farmer's wife and be taking care of the children while [he] was in the field making a living." But her fate would be different. Like millions of other African

Women who worked in the fields usually were responsible for housework as well.

Americans at different times and in different places, Minnie Savage watched her hopes wither.

When the entry of the United States into World War I in 1917 took her brothers into the army, she knew that her dreams would once again be sacrificed to the reality of her family's dependence on her labor. For 16-year-old Minnie, the only alternative seemed to be an entirely different route, and she headed for Philadelphia, where she had a cousin willing to help her get settled in a new home. "I didn't know nothing about the city," she later recalled. "I had never dreamed about being in the city."

Poorly educated and "green," Minnie had difficulties at first. Her cousin's contacts yielded a job in a drugstore, but a task as simple as writing down names of people who called on the telephone tested the limits of her literacy. By the early 1920s she was working as a maid, scrubbing floors for an employer who insisted that a mop would not do as well as a hand brush. But as hard as the work was, and although in many ways Philadelphia was as segregated as Virginia, this was not the South. On one visit to her parents, she recalled,

> [I] was standin' on my porch and the white man came up and said to my father, "I want some of your people to come and pick strawberries for me." So Poppa told him that he doesn't have any, that his boys is workin' and he needs them. So he looked at me and said "What about her? Isn't she one of your gals?" Poppa said, "She doesn't live here." So he says, "What's the difference?" And that's when I opened my mouth and said, "No indeed. I don't live here no more. I was born here, but I don't come down here to work. I could give you a job!"

Returning South was not an alternative. But New York, which Minnie (now Minnie Savage Whitney, after a brief marriage) had already visited, was. In 1929 she moved to Harlem and found a job in a laundry.

There is no such thing as a "typical" biography. For most individuals, life twists and turns distinctively—although frequently in ways that provide hints and insights into broader patterns of history. Minnie Savage Whitney's first three decades are striking in this regard. Her story, although it tells the life of only a single individual, highlights broad themes and sensibilities central to African-American life during the first three decades of the 20th century. In 1900, 90 percent of all African Americans lived in the South; three-fourths of these 8 million people inhabited rural communities. The 880,771 black Northerners, on the other hand, were decidedly urban; 71 percent lived in cities.

Wherever they lived, most African Americans worked long hours and made little money for their efforts. Like Minnie, black women were more likely than their white counterparts to work outside their own homes. Also like Minnie, approximately 1.5 million African Americans moved north between 1916 and 1930. This massive exodus, known as the "Great Migration," continued through the 1960s and transformed American cities, African-American culture, and virtually all aspects of American society and politics.

Minnie's rebuff of a white Southerner's claim to the right to call on a black woman's labor—"I don't live here no more"—reflected the assertive attitude common among African Americans who chose to leave the South in the 1910s and 1920s. Migration to the North was at once a rejection of a way of life and a vision of new possibilities—"a chance to make good," as one black Southerner put it just before leaving. Once they had arrived in Northern cities, black Southerners were likely to encounter both the disappointments and the opportunities later recalled by Minnie Savage Whitney.

Black travelers were confined to the segregated waiting room of the Jacksonville, Florida, train station. The Supreme Court's decision in Plessy v. Ferguson *upheld "separate but equal" public facilities.*

Writer, editor, activist, teacher, and social scientist, W. E. B. Du Bois stands as one of the intellectual giants of the twentieth century.

At the time of Minnie Savage's birth, another African American was beginning to make his mark as a leading intellectual and social reformer. W. E. B. Du Bois's 1903 observation that "the problem of the Twentieth Century is the problem of the color line" has been quoted so often as to become a cliché, a shorthand reference to the overriding importance of racism in American society.

Born in Massachusetts in 1868, Du Bois had earned a B.A. from Fisk University and a Ph.D. from Harvard in addition to studying at the University of Berlin. A brilliant and prolific social scientist, he would later become equally notable—and eminently quotable—as an activist, writer, and public intellectual. He also would come to an understanding of American history and culture that emphasized that racism did not exist in a vacuum. Du Bois recognized that it was impossible to understand the meaning of race without also understanding class. The place of African Americans in American society was inseparable from their place in the economy.

Moreover, as Minnie Savage Whitney's experience demonstrates, the African-American experience in the 20th century has also been closely intertwined with the significance of gender. Just as the term *race* refers to the meaning that we attach to skin color, *gender* refers to the meaning a society attaches to manhood and womanhood. The life to which the young Minnie Savage aspired in the rural South—to "be taking care of the children" in the house while her spouse worked the fields—would not have been the dream of very many (if any at all) black men—or white men for that matter. Minnie's sense of who she was, who she would like to be, and during the course of her life, who she actually could be, had much to do with deeply rooted social conventions regarding gender.

History and personal experience taught African Americans that their position in American society could not be understood without understanding racism. But race was not the only basis for discrimination in American life. Nor was it the only way Americans defined who they were and why they were different from other people. Class and gender, along with religion, the ethnic group to which a person belonged, and age, also shaped lives, ideas, and dreams.

Perhaps the problem of the 20th century has indeed been the "color line." But the significance and the composition of that line cannot be reduced to the biology of skin pigmentation. The meaning of race, and the practice of racism, were tightly intertwined with labor systems, ideas about family life, and assumptions about the relationship between manhood and citizenship.

This book explores the lives of African Americans in early-20th–century America. It begins in the midst of a period that was described in one classic historical study as the "nadir," the low point, of post–Civil War African-American history. And in many ways this was indeed a time of defeat, destitution, and despair. If freed slaves had expected in 1865 to enter the ranks of independent landowning farmers, their descendants who came of age a generation later instead watched their parents struggle to work a crop owned by a white landlord. If emancipated slaves had envisioned freedom as a status entitling them to the rights of full citizenship, their children would watch state constitutional conventions and legislatures during the 1890s systematically strip them of meaningful access to the political system and legal institutions.

Black teenage girls grew into adulthood with the knowledge that it was virtually impossible to get a Southern jury to convict a white man of rape if the victim was a black woman. In Southern cities, black men were pushed out of skilled trades in which they had previously maintained a foothold, at the same time that they were being denied jobs in new industries. Congress had turned its back on Reconstruction in 1876, when the last federal troops were withdrawn from the South. By the end of the century the Supreme Court had confirmed the federal government's abdication of its responsibility to nearly half of all American citizens in the South. Court rulings such as *Plessy* v. *Ferguson* left Reconstruction-era civil rights legislation utterly toothless, while upholding limitations on the right of black Southerners to vote and laws that required racial segregation.

In the North, despite the absence of legal constraints, a set of ideas that emphasized racial differences increasingly came to dominate white people's assumptions about how societies naturally organize themselves. The number of blacks who held elective office and joined labor unions had increased in the 1880s, only to decline in the following decade. When black and white workers crossed picket lines, enraged white labor union members were likely to point their fingers (and occasionally weapons) at black strikebreakers—workers whose only access to many jobs was through

As more and more blacks moved to Northern cities, they found themselves forced to live in crowded ghettos like this one in Philadelphia.

strikebreaking. What had once been a set of small black enclaves in Northern cities, or even merely concentrations of black residents on particular blocks, began to become ghettos, as whites moved out of mixed neighborhoods and resisted the movement of blacks into predominantly white areas.

The trends were evident even in American foreign policy, as the United States joined Europe in taking up what was then called "the white man's burden" in the Philippines, Hawaii, Puerto Rico, and Haiti. In part because they were not properly Christian, and in part because they were not properly white—important indications of levels of civilization—the inhabitants of these countries were considered by many Americans to be incapable of self-government.

Textbooks and atlases reflected these assumptions. These books organized the world around the "great races," each of which had particular characteristics—including a place in a pecking order that implied that higher levels of civilization corresponded with light skin and residence in the Northern Hemisphere. "It was dark days for black people when I was born into this world in 1906," remarked teacher and civil rights activist Lyman Johnson, recalling his childhood in Tennessee

As bad as things were, however, this picture of unceasing toil, victimization, and disappointment tells only a part of the story. There was disappointment because there was hope. In the South blacks were deprived of the vote and forced into racial segregation in part because of the threats posed by African Americans who refused to accept second-class citizenship. Many whites thought that these young men and women had to be controlled because they would not behave properly; they did not seem to know their "place." They would not conform to expectations held by white Southerners, expectations closely related to a powerful myth of a "golden age" before the Civil War when paternalistic slaveowners supposedly had presided over what these masters had called their "family, white and black."

Many white Southerners believed that slavery had worked so well (and slaves supposedly been so loyal) because African Americans were naturally suited to taking orders from whites, either on the farm or around the kitchen. Black Southerners had always resisted, but in comparison with the old dependable "darky" who inhabited the "golden age" myth, the new generation seemed threatening to whites. Washerwomen went on strike in Atlanta. Cotton pickers joined the Colored Farmers Alliance. Workers in Richmond joined the Knights of Labor. Employing less direct modes of resistance, household servants continued to insist on their "tote," a share of food to take home to their own families.

Hope lay not only in traditions of African-American resistance that dated back to slavery. Many black Southerners also drew strength from a sense of individual and group accomplishment. Measured against 1865— as many black Americans at the time viewed their past and present—they had made impressive progress. In 1900 in the South, although most black farmers remained mired in tenancy, 179,000 African Americans owned more than 11 million acres of land. The quest for land embodied a continued faith that land ownership was related to both citizenship and independence. It also implied self-confidence in farming skills and insistence on the right to own land.

Similarly, the continuing struggle for black schools rested on community values that honored education and accepted sacrifice in the name of future generations. In the North black lawyers and doctors were few and far between, but were more numerous than ever before. In the South, even the most racist white school officials were increasingly apt to hire African Americans to teach in black schools, primarily because they could be paid considerably less than white teachers. In Northern and Southern cities a growing African-American business class served the emerging ghettos.

These black communities had deep roots in the black churches, schools, and fraternal societies that had emerged in American cities before the Civil War. By the end of the 19th century, black newspapers had been started in nearly all major cities. Indeed, the best way for the modern reader to "visit" a turn-of-the-century black community is to read these newspapers.

The black women's club movement reached maturity during this period. Their role in the development of orphanages, shelters for newly arrived women, and homes for the elderly exemplified their commitment to the motto of the National Association of Colored Women: "lifting as we climb." Similarly for black men, membership in the lodges of the Knights of Pythias, Prince Hall Masons, Oddfellows, or numerous other fraternal societies provided sociability and conveyed a degree of respectability as a member of the community. In Chicago and New York, a political elite was emerging, as consolidation of African-American areas of residence laid the basis for mobilizing voting power.

These kinds of community-building activities rested on a strong sense of solidarity within black communities. These communities simultaneously required and nurtured their own leadership class. Many community leaders were children or grandchildren of slaves. Robert Graves Johnson, principal of the "Negro school" in Columbia, Tennessee, raised his children in the early 20th century in a small house that included the one-room log cabin that his father had built soon after purchasing his freedom a decade before the Civil War. Men and women who could recall

being owned as slaves could watch as their children moved into business, professional occupations, or land ownership. This sense of history and progress sustained hope among those who had managed these modest levels of achievement.

History. Progress. Hope. The relationship between these themes has for generations provided a focus for American textbooks, Fourth of July orations, and Presidential addresses. This notion of history as a relentless march forward toward a greater tomorrow, however, has been less self-evident to African Americans.

In African-American history, images of victimization spring to mind as readily as notions of progress. Hope has most often bred disappointment, and frequently disillusionment as well. This book presents a history of Americans who shared in the aspirations and expectations of their fellow

Membership in clubs offered many urban blacks opportunities to take leadership roles in community affairs.

citizens, but who did so as people with a unique history and a unique set of barriers to overcome.

African Americans argued among themselves as to what those barriers were made of; exactly where they were situated; how permanent they were; and whether they should be destroyed, circumvented, or hurdled. During the first three decades of the 20th century thousands of black men and women obliterated, removed, tiptoed around, climbed over, and even passed through these barriers. Others ignored them. Some resigned themselves to the limitations and pain these barriers produced, without accepting the notion that the barriers were either natural or just. And still others suffered from the costs of pounding the barriers at times and in places where they were too deeply embedded in the social fabric to be breached.

This is the story of those who attacked these barriers and those who adapted themselves to the obstacles they encountered. It is the story of Minnie Savage and W. E. B. Du Bois and countless others who lived in this time of hope and age of despair.

CHAPTER 1

MAKING A LIVING
◇ ◇ ◇

At the dawn of the 20th century the color line, or the separation between whites and blacks, was most clear and most rigid in the South. With 95 percent of African Americans living south of the Ohio River and east of central Texas, this was also where the overwhelming majority of black people lived. Before the Civil War, the Ohio River and the Mason–Dixon line (separating Pennsylvania from Maryland) had marked the line between slavery and freedom—even though "freedom" in the North was limited by employment discrimination, barriers to voting and officeholding, and racial segregation.

In 1900, 35 years after emancipation, this boundary remained particularly meaningful to African Americans. South of the line, citizenship guaranteed little. To describe the condition of blacks in the South, both whites and blacks used a phrase first articulated by the United States Supreme Court in 1857 (*Dred Scott* v. *Sanford*, known as the "Dred Scott decision") to limit the scope of African-American citizenship before the Civil War: blacks had "no rights which the white man was bound to respect." That was still the case in the South in 1900.

In the North, black men and women enjoyed the same legal rights as whites, but an informal color line set the races apart, limiting where blacks could work, live, and send their children to school. In the West, patterns somewhat resembled the North. In both regions African Americans lived mainly in cities. Because the black populations in Western states remained small, however, there tended to be greater flexibility and fewer restrictions. Indeed, blacks not only were barely visible in the West, but in many cases attracted less hostility than Asian and Mexican immigrants. "There wasn't

Several generations harvest the tobacco crop on a farm in Doerum, Georgia. Tobacco ranked second to cotton as a cash crop among African-American farmers in the South.

23

an awful lot of prejudice," recalled an African-American resident of Seattle; nor was there "an awful lot of opportunities either."

Despite these significant variations, however, racism had become a part of American national culture. African Americans everywhere were likely to earn less than whites, work longer hours at less desirable jobs (or be unemployed), and confront limitations on where they could go and what they could do. The story of the 20th century begins where the restrictions were the most concrete and wide ranging, and where most African Americans lived and worked: in the South.

As the century opened, four-fifths of all black Southerners lived in rural communities. Most were members of families who earned their living from the land. What they planted depended largely on where they lived. Tobacco remained important in Virginia, North Carolina, and Kentucky. Sugarcane continued to be grown in Louisiana. Through most of the South cotton still reigned. But whatever they grew and wherever they lived, most African Americans across the South worked, worshipped, rested, and partied around cycles of labor—the long hours required to plant, cultivate, and harvest a cash crop (a crop grown to be sold rather than to be consumed by the household). And most operated within a system of land ownership and rental that varied considerably in its details but little in its basic framework.

Since emancipation most black Southerners had envisioned land ownership as the key to freedom. As one black soldier explained at the end of

Man and ox on a Newport News, Virginia, farm at the turn of the century. Because Southern cotton and tobacco farms mechanized later than farms in other regions of the United States, animals remained essential.

the Civil War, "Every colored man will be a slave, & feel himself a slave until he can raise him own bale of cotton & put him own mark upon it & say dis is mine!" By 1900, approximately one-fourth of all black Southerners who operated farms owned the soil they tilled. The number of black farm owners—and their total acreage—increased each year. Southern black leaders frequently pointed to these accomplishments as evidence of a strong work ethic among their people and of the great potential that lay in the rural South.

But the story was more complicated and less encouraging than the tale told by these statistics. Impressive increases in total acreage owned by black Southerners did testify to hard work and frugality. Many lived according to the work ethic later articulated by Alabama farmer Ned Cobb: "I didn't come in this world to rust out. If I need anything done in my field I ought to be there if time will admit it, on time. I got to work. I'm born to work."

In the opening decades of the 20th century Cobb clawed his way up the ladder from wage laborer to sharecropper, cash renter, and finally owner. But he never was able to accumulate much, and more than once he was cheated out of his assets by white landlords or merchants. For him, as so many others, prosperity—even mere independence—remained a difficult goal to achieve and maintain.

These farms were small and seldom grew any larger. Moreover even farmers who had not borrowed money to purchase their farms still needed some form of credit to meet a year's expenses before their crop could be harvested in the fall. Partly because the land worked by black farmers tended to be worth less than the crop that could be grown on it, local merchants and bankers would secure loans by taking a lien on the crop (a guarantee they would have first rights to the sale of the crop) rather than a mortgage on the land. Instead of repossessing the land if a farmer failed to repay, the lender (lienholder) took what was due out of the sale of the crop. The farmer got what was left, and sometimes that was very little.

The holder of the lien could (and often did) require that the farmer put most of his fields into a cash crop in order to increase the likelihood of the farmer repaying his debt. Families who owned land thus had to purchase food that they otherwise might have grown themselves—and often from the same merchant who demanded that as a condition of their loan they plant most of their fields in cotton or tobacco.

With little money to invest, and working on land that was less productive than that available to renters, most black farm owners maintained an unstable grip on their independence. One or two years of bad weather or low prices for their crops could hurl them back into tenancy (that is, farming a plot of land owned by someone else). The symbolic value of ownership, and the extent to which it permitted members of the family to go about their lives without thinking about a white landlord, could only multiply the pain of losing one's land.

The vast majority of black farmers rented their land. Rental could take two forms: cash rent or sharecropping. Cash renters paid a specified sum to operate a farm on a particular piece of land. Owning only their work animals and their tools, they were even more likely than owners to sacrifice control over their crop by borrowing money for living expenses in return for a lien. But even if they were debtors, cash renters were not completely at the beck and call of their landlords. Families could make their own decisions about who would work in the fields and who might work in the home or go to school. What they grew belonged to them, and they used the proceeds to settle their debts. If they had a good crop and prices were high, they might benefit from their skill and good fortune.

Most black tenants, however, were sharecroppers, especially where cotton was the main crop. Although there were many variations of share tenancy, certain patterns were common, in part because of the peculiar legal arrangements. Landlord and tenant signed a contract that usually ran from January 1 through December 31. Generally the landlord received half of the cotton and one-third of the corn, although the proportion of the cotton, especially, could vary according to who provided mules and farm implements.

Unlike cash renters, sharecroppers did not own their crop; it belonged to their landlords, who paid them their share after harvest and sale. A sharecropper, unlike a wage laborer, received no cash payment for labor as it was being performed. This meant that most sharecroppers had no source of money until the end of the year. They had to borrow—either from the landlord or from a local merchant—in order to meet normal family expenses. These loans (often called "furnish") would be repaid after "settlement." Settlement took place at the end of the year, when the landlord (or merchant) would compare the value of the tenant's portion of the crop with the sum "advanced" to the tenant during the preceding twelve months.

Almost invariably the sharecropper came out either behind or barely even. Even the thousands of sharecroppers who were illiterate and therefore unable to challenge the accounting suspected that they seldom

Children provided an essential supplement to their parents when it came time to pick cotton. Schools for African-American children in the South closed when the bolls ripened.

received their due. In 1919, for example, George Conway of Keo, Arkansas, raised 20 bales of cotton, worth $3,500. Although he knew that he had not purchased more than $300 worth of merchandise on credit from his landlord that year, he was told at settlement that he still owed $40. His demand for an itemized accounting earned him only a beating. Still claiming a debt of $40, the landlord seized Conway's household goods and drove him off the plantation.

The inevitability of the unfair settlement became a staple of African-American humor, with innumerable variations of a joke that has a tenant secretly withholding a bale or two of cotton at settlement time. He watches the landlord go through the customary calculations of the value of the crop and the sharecropper's debt, yielding the seemingly inevitable result that the cotton would bring just enough to settle the debt—leaving the sharecropper with nothing to show for his year's labor. The sharecropper then triumphantly produces the extra cotton and waits eagerly for a calculation of his profits. Instead the landlord scratches his head and chides the sharecropper for forcing him to sit down again with pencil and paper to redo the calculations to produce the same result. As William Pickens, whose family sharecropped in South Carolina and Arkansas, later observed, "Who could deny it? The white man did all the reckoning. The Negro did all the work."

To complain or to threaten legal action was useless; no court would rule in favor of a black sharecropper against a white landlord. A sharecropper could carry over a debt into the next year; move to another farm with the debt built into the next contract; or quietly try to leave—to skip out on an obligation that most black Southerners considered a complete sham anyway.

Indeed the debt was even worse than a sham. By law the tenant was actually a wage laborer; the crop belonged to the landlord. But the landlord had it both ways. The sharecropper family worked, yet received no regular wages. They were paid nothing until the crop had been harvested and sold. Thus the landlord was actually the one who should have been considered the debtor. The cash—or wage—that was being withheld from the laborer was a debt, cash that the landlord owed the tenant but did not have to pay until December.

To satisfy the basic needs of their families, sharecroppers thus had to borrow at high interest rates, generally ranging from 40 to 70 percent in an era when rates elsewhere generally fluctuated between 4 and 8 percent. Even at these outrageous prices, sharecroppers could get credit to buy only what the landlord (or furnishing merchant) deemed appropriate.

Those basic needs were quite modest. The standard of living among black sharecroppers in the South was generally lower than that of mid-19th-century westward pioneers. But where the pioneers' log cabins suggest to us images of upwardly mobile families clearing homesteads and carving out a living from the land, sharecroppers' log cabins represent a very different reality. These cabins, which could be constructed out of rough boards rather than logs, were dark, sometimes without windows. Where there were openings they generally lacked glass panes, and often even shutters as well. Screens were virtually unknown. Keeping the house clean, considered to be women's work, was virtually impossible.

With only three rooms or less, it was equally impossible to create specialized spaces for such activities as eating, sleeping, or memorizing one's school lessons. Several members of a family slept in a single room, with five or more not at all uncommon. At a time when middle- and upper-class Americans had come to expect divisions between "private" and "public" spaces in their homes, the tenant's cabin afforded no such luxury. There was no such thing as a room that had only one purpose or was the domain of a single family member.

A black sharecropper and his large family outside their window-less Albany, Georgia, cabin. Most such cabins had only one or two rooms in which families cooked, slept, and ate. These homes were hot in the summer and almost impossible to heat in the winter.

For many sharecroppers, family life was different from that idealized by a "mainstream" middle-class family. Black families in the rural South resembled the two-parent households common elsewhere in the United States at the time, but were more likely to include older relatives as well. Perhaps the presence of other adults left husbands and fathers with less authority than their counterparts elsewhere. Many definitely had to share authority with their landlords, who drew contracts that permitted them to require family members to work the fields. Black men thus came to value their ability to relieve their wives and children of field work. Moreover, by controlling the "furnish," a landlord could influence relations within a sharecropper's family by defining the range of purchasing options—how much of each kind of clothing, how many luxuries, or what kind of food.

The sharecropper's diet was dull and often sparse. A garden could yield plenty of food, but many landlords required their tenants to grow cotton almost to the door. The Delta Farm Company, owner of 35,000 acres of land in Mound Bayou County, Mississippi, for example, prohibited its tenants from raising anything other than cotton. No chickens or vegetables were permitted. Generally, tenants tended small gardens, supplemented by what they could afford at the local store. The result was a lot of cornmeal and poor cuts of pork, all prepared with generous quantities of animal fat—another challenge to women who increasingly were being told by agricultural reformers (black and white) to be better housewives by preparing more healthful food.

Indeed, the growing movements for better farming methods and more efficient rural housekeeping bore little relevance to the realities of sharecropping. There was no incentive for tenants or owners to improve either the farm or the dwelling. Landlords were steeped in a culture committed to an agricultural economy based on cheap labor. They also were steeped in a culture which assumed that black people would have difficulty learning advanced farming methods or how to operate and maintain machinery. Landlords considered mules and cabins appropriate to the aptitudes and productivity of African Americans. A greater investment in equipment or living conditions, they thought, would neither raise the value of their property nor increase output. Moreover, the landlord would receive only a portion of any increased yield that might result from improvement.

On the tenant's side, improving the farm made even less sense. Why invest sweat or money into a home or farm that was owned by someone else? What little cash a family might accumulate was best spent in

The washing machine of the 1920s was a woman with a washboard and tub. Black families frequently took in whites' laundry in addition to their own to supplement their incomes.

moveable items that could increase one's share of the crop next time around: a wagon, a mule, or a plow. And why accumulate household goods when in all likelihood the family would move within a few years? Little surprise that housekeeping technology seldom went far beyond water pail, washtub, and cooking kettle.

Having no investment in home or farm, and encountering constant frustration regardless of how hard they worked, sharecroppers were bound to remain alert to other possibilities. Perhaps this 20 acres might be slightly better than that plot. Perhaps this landlord might be less inclined to cheat at settlement time—or less inclined to pressure wife and children to work in the fields. Conversely, as children grew and contributed more in the fields, it made sense to find a landlord who would permit more acreage to be farmed.

While many families remained on a single farm for years, William Pickens's parents, who sharecropped in South Carolina and Arkansas, were more typical. By the time he had reached his 19th birthday in 1900 he had known more than 20 buildings that he could call "home." "My parents were farmers of the tenant or day-labor class and were ever on the move from cabin to cabin," he later recalled.

At first they moved locally, from farm to farm within their rural South Carolina community. Their big chance seemed to strike in the late 1880s, when a visitor told them about Arkansas, where planters were clamoring for men to work land being brought under cultivation. The man was a "labor agent," one of many recruiters who in the late 19th century traveled through those parts of the South where years of growing cotton or tobacco had worn the land thin.

These agents worked for planters further south in Florida or—more frequently—further west in the Mississippi Delta or in Arkansas. With no prospects in South Carolina, Pickens's parents were prepared to listen. "The agent said that Arkansas was a tropical country of soft and balmy air, where coconuts, oranges, lemons, and bananas grew. Ordinary things like corn and cotton, with little cultivation, grew an enormous yield." Similar stories of recruitment come from Georgia and North Carolina, where men and women facing a future as bleak as the Pickens', heard tales of rich Mississippi bottomland, soil so fertile it barely had to be plowed.

So they went. During the last two decades of the 19th century and the first decade of the 20th, the system stabilized but people moved. The South's black population churned as rural people moved from plantation to plantation, county to county, state to state in quest of the holy grail of land ownership. Some, like the Pickenses, were lured by labor agents. Others, especially in hilly areas where whites already outnumbered blacks, were pushed out in a process known as "whitecapping," a term that referred to the practice of night riders pushing African Americans off their land through threat of violence. At least 239 instances of whitecapping were recorded during the two decades beginning in the late 1880s, with Mississippi the most common site. Night riding was popular in Georgia, Tennessee, and Alabama as well. The term seems to have originated in Indiana, where night riders invading a small community or threatening an individual African-American resident would wear white caps as part of their disguise.

Despite its origins in the Midwest, whitecapping was mainly a Southern rural phenomenon. Successful black farmers were the most likely target of this kind of eviction because of the common assumption among whites that the success of some blacks might unleash unrealistic (and dangerous) aspirations among the local black population. A farmer in Alpharetta, Georgia, recognized that he "better not accumulate much, no matter how hard and honest you work for it, as they—well, you can't enjoy it." In some cases, whole communities were forced from their homes. Black farmers would find signs posted on roads warning them to leave or face

Graffiti on the rock wall separating Edwards and Kimble Counties in Texas indicates that blacks were not welcome in either location. R.S. stands for Rock Springs, in Edwards, and J.C. for Junction City, in Kimble.

dire consequences, or white men would appear at their doors with rifles and the message that they had 24 hours to leave the county. In one Georgia county signs were posted on the black schoolhouse and elsewhere that blacks would no longer be permitted to live "from the river north of the town to the Blue Ridge Mountains."

In areas more heavily populated by African Americans, especially the "Black Belt" stretching across the cotton-growing region of South Carolina, Georgia, Alabama, Mississippi, Louisiana, and East Texas, nature took its toll as well. The boll weevil, an insect that devoured cotton, entered the United States from Mexico toward the end of the 19th century. Moving east, it left in its wake a devastation aptly summarized by a piece of cotton field verse:

> De white man he got ha'f de crop
> Boll-weevil took de res'.
> Ain't got no home.
> Ain't got no home.

Some landlords responded by diversifying their farms, especially after 1910, when the weevil's impact interacted with a growing agricultural reform movement. Corn required only one-fifth as much labor as cotton, which meant that many black tenants and wage hands were suddenly thrown out of work. In other cases black farmers confronted with a weevil-infested crop headed for areas rumored to be untouched, or abandoned farming altogether.

This constant movement vexed landlords, but it was virtually built into the system. Indeed, contrary to conventional opinion among whites, the proclivity to move had little to do with what whites called "Negro character." Black Southerners did move more frequently than whites, but mainly because they were more likely to be sharecroppers—the most mobile category of farmers. Among all sharecroppers in the early-20th-century South, African Americans had the lowest rates of mobility; black cash renters and owners were each more stable than their white counterparts. Although some of this motion was caused either by white terrorism or a decline in the demand for black labor, most black Southerners moved of their own accord. As one black Mississippian explained, "Whenever we get an opportunity and inducement and [are] in position to take care of ourself, we moves."

This was, in fact, the American way. The movement of labor toward opportunity is essential to the efficient operation of labor markets in a growing economy. Free labor implies the ability of workers to move from depressed locales to areas of expansion, liberating both the worker to take advantage of opportunity and the employer from any responsibility for supporting former employees.

But the rural South, especially where cotton or sugar cultivation dominated patterns of employment, was committed to a different type of economy—one dominated by the plantation, a form of production that required a tightly controlled labor force. Except in areas where new lands were being brought into cultivation, a stable labor force seemed essential to both the prosperity of individual landowners and the stability of the system itself. Complaints about a "chaotic" labor market and "restless" and "unreliable" black labor abounded. White landowners lamented the inclination of their tenants to be "controlled far more by their fancies than by their common sense."

In response, nearly all Southern states, and many localities as well, attempted to immobilize black labor by erecting legal and economic barriers to movement. Although enmeshed in a capitalist economy based on the ability of the employer to purchase—and control—only the *labor* of workers, and not the workers themselves, Southern landlords insisted on their right to limit the ability of people they called "their negroes" to change employers.

Control over land and credit provided the basis for one set of barriers to mobility. Many landowners limited the amount of land they would rent to each tenant in order to ensure that the sharecropper would cultivate the land intensively. Moreover, tenants with small plots were less likely to earn enough to permit them to advance into the ranks of landowners. One Southern landowner readily admitted that he would not rent more than 10 acres to a family regardless of how many workers the household could supply because "the soil was so productive" that "they would soon be making such a profit that they would be able to buy a farm of their own."

The goal was to keep black Southerners as dependent as possible on white landowners and merchants. Where the sharecropper was not dependent he could be tied down by contract. In most Southern states a sharecropping contract differed from most other contracts in that it was enforceable in criminal rather than civil courts. A sharecropper who skipped out after planting a crop would not be sued (he was not likely to have any assets anyway), but arraigned on criminal charges.

A Mississippi planter made no bones about either his willingness or ability to maintain his claim on a restless tenant: "If he goes away, I just go

Children learned the techniques of cotton farming from their parents. The schedule of planting, cultivating, and harvesting the cotton determined family cycles of work and recreation.

and get him." In most cases the level and method of compulsion stopped short of peonage—defined as forcibly keeping a laborer in place beyond a contract period. Most debtors were permitted to move, carrying their debt from place to place, or were simply let go after the creditor seized their personal property to satisfy the debt.

Indeed, what really mattered was not whether a tenant remained on a particular farm so much as whether a locality's total labor force remained stable. Local movement was expected and tolerated. Indeed, local movement provided frustrated and discontented tenants with an apparent choice of options, a reason to hope that a new chance might yield a better crop and brighter future. What was crucial was to limit the threat to the local labor supply, to assure that come picking time there would be enough black men, women, and children to drag heavy sacks through the fields.

Assuming (incorrectly) that long-distance movement was largely the result of smooth-tongued recruiters, Southern landlords and employers went to considerable lengths to curb the "labor agent menace." "There are farmers," declared Georgia recruiter Peg Leg Williams, "that would not hesitate to shoot their brother were he to come from Mississippi to get 'his niggers,' as he calls them." States and localities across the South put considerable effort into keeping "their negroes" ignorant of outside opportunities.

In 1900 the United States Supreme Court for the first time upheld the constitutionality of the laws requiring labor agents to pay licensing fees that were so high as to make it impossible to legally entice away a community's black workers. A flood of legislation followed, as state and local governments determined to protect their labor force from recruiters.

Recruitment laws had little effect, however. They were extremely difficult to enforce. Even more important, they ignored the influence of informal networks across the black South that carried information—and misinformation—about opportunities in developing sections of the region. What really kept black Southerners in place kept them not in particular communities, but in the regional economy as a whole: there were few alternatives—at least for men—beyond seasonal farm work. As the *Pee Dee Watchman,* a South Carolina black newspaper, explained in 1917, since the end of Reconstruction in the 1870s, "thousands desired to leave but could find no haven, no place where the demand for negro labor was greater than the supply."

Moreover, within the rural economy opportunities existed for employment during the slack season. A cotton crop requires spurts of intense activity—preparing the field, planting, hoeing, and harvesting—punctuated by intervals of monitoring. These intervals permitted family members who did not have primary responsibility for a crop to seek other employment.

Turpentine camps, sawmills, cottonseed-oil mills, and other industries tied to the rural economy provided young men with opportunities to earn cash wages. Young women ventured into cities and towns to earn extra cash washing, cooking, or cleaning. In most cases these individuals moved back and forth between town (or less frequently, city) and farm, with the longest interval coming after picking in the late fall and before planting time in March.

Leaving the countryside permanently, however, was a more daunting matter, especially for men. The new and expanding industries of the early-20th-century South offered few opportunities to black workers. Textiles, furniture, oil and gas, paper, chemicals—each contributed to the growth of Southern cities and southern factories, each was interested only in white people as machine tenders.

Skilled positions in such new urban sectors as electrical production and streetcar transportation remained equally off-limits, while at the same time white workers were displacing blacks from 19th-century footholds in the skilled construction trades. Black men could find jobs in coal mines and in the iron and steel mills in the area of Birmingham, Alabama. But these

Cincinnati construction workers attach a streetcar rail to the railbed. By 1910, approximately 130,000 African Americans earned a living working on the railroad.

represented exceptions to the general pattern of casual employment known as "negro labor." The urban economy thus meshed effectively with the rural. The plantation needed a stable labor force that could find outlets during slack periods; town and city employers looked to black workers to fill temporary needs usually involving a shovel or a broom.

Black women, on the other hand, had little difficulty finding urban employment as long as they were willing to work for a pittance. Middle- and upper-class white southerners expected black women to do their domestic chores. Wages for domestic workers were so low that even many white workers considered the availability of black "help" a part of their birthright. In contrast to Northern cities, where black servants were part of a labor market that included a large component of white European immigrants, Southern households invariably employed African Americans. And in contrast to a widespread pattern of live-in service among those immigrants, black women generally insisted on living at home. "They seem to think that it is something against their freedom if they sleep where they are employed," observed one employer whose dismissal of this sentiment stands in stark contrast to its accuracy. Nevertheless, in addition to a customary 12–14-hour day, black women domestic workers often had to respond to demands for extra hours.

The servant's day was not only long, it was physically and emotionally difficult. Only servants for the wealthiest families could specialize as cook

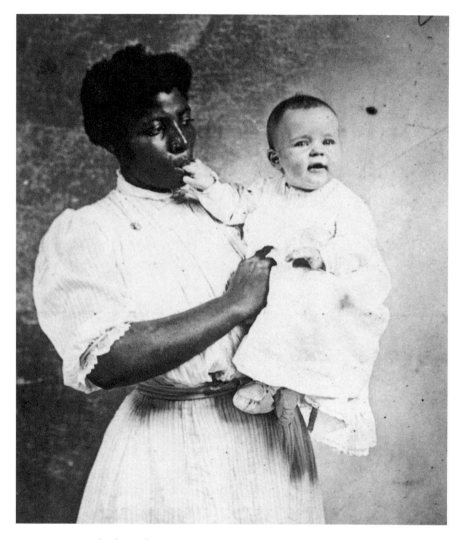

Domestic service was the most frequent occupation for black women who worked outside the home in both North and South. But they preferred the independence of day work to live-in employment.

or nurse. "I'm looking for a nurse for my children," usually implied cleaning, cooking, and serving as well. That nurse also had to fight for her dignity in a household where as one woman noted, "The child I work for calls me girl." The man of the house could (and often did) present a very different kind of threat to a servant's dignity—pressure for sexual favors. One servant explained that she lost a job when "I refused to let the madam's husband kiss me. . . . He walked up to me, threw his arms around me, and was in the act of kissing me, when I demanded to know what he meant, and shoved him away." When the black woman's husband filed a complaint against her employer, he was arrested and fined $25.

Resistance to the regimen and the disrespect, however, was often more subtle than a generally useless formal complaint. Taking advantage of whites' assumptions about black women's carelessness, servants would appear to be careless. A hot iron purposely left too long on a garment could provide a fitting revenge against an employer who refused to permit a servant to take a quick trip home to visit her own children. Similarly, servants would invent holidays that their employers would grudgingly acknowledge. Whites chalked the festival up to "negro character" (they would never have used the word "culture")—something which they could never understand and felt was not worth figuring out anyway.

A woman who wanted a little more control over her time, especially to take care of her own family, would clean other people's clothes rather than their homes. The work was hard, and only slightly more remunerative than domestic service. And taking in laundry carried risks: one ruined or lost garment could bring a refusal to pay for a whole load. Like the sharecroppers whose landlord refused to pay a proper settlement, a laundress had no recourse to the courts when a dispute arose. Remarkably, washerwomen and domestics did strike, in some cases maintaining considerable solidarity. But the deck was stacked against any permanent shift in the balance of power between these women and their employers. Most women even preferred picking cotton to domestic work (it paid better), and white women in towns and cities across the "cotton belt" complained—or raised wages—when ripening cotton bolls attracted their servants to the countryside.

Residents of towns and cities were unlikely to find the countryside unfamiliar. Many had come from farms in the first place. Moreover, black urban neighborhoods in the South showed little evidence of the outpouring of services undertaken by cities of this era. African Americans generally lived on unpaved streets where such standard urban services as police, fire protection, garbage collection, and sewers were rare. As late as the mid-1920s Monroe Work, director of research at Tuskegee Institute in Alabama, could describe most of the Southern urban black population as living under "country conditions . . . just beyond the zones for water, lights, and other conveniences." Infant mortality was high, as were stillbirths. In this, as in so many other ways, the black South remained a rural world even as the proportion living in cities rose gradually from 15 percent in 1890 to 21 percent 20 years later.

By the second decade of the 20th century, cotton cultivation still employed more black Southerners than any other single activity. Men awoke at dawn and headed to the fields. Women awoke even earlier to prepare breakfast—sometimes eaten in the cabin and sometimes in the fields, where women often worked alongside their husbands. The two major slack periods in the cotton cycle—July and August, when the weeds had been hoed and the plants could be left with minimal attention, and the last two months of the year, after the cotton bolls had been picked—provided rural black Southerners with opportunities for leisure.

The first of these periods coincided with food harvests. Barbecues, religious revivals, and other community gatherings were common summer activities. The later months followed "settlement"; what little cash was realized from a year's labor could be devoted to generally secular Christmas celebrations, shopping either in town or from a mail-order catalog, and contemplating a change of scenery. Well into the 1920s, the rhythms of the black South synchronized with the patterns of cotton cultivation.

The black North and West, on the other hand, were distinctly urban. Cities housed 70 percent of all black Northerners and 67 percent of black Westerners at the turn of the century. By 1910 the urbanized portion of the black population in both regions was close to 80 percent. As they did in the South, women were most likely to find work as domestic servants. Men occasionally had access to industrial jobs, but usually only as temporary strikebreakers replacing white unionists.

A small business class, complemented by an even smaller group of professionals, constituted the upper class in these communities. Craftsmen had difficulties finding employment, especially in cities with strong unions in the building trades, which generally excluded African-American workmen. In some cities, most notably on the West Coast, black men in such occupations as hotel waiters and bellmen were losing their jobs to immigrants from abroad. For most men, the tools of the trade all too often remained the familiar shovel, broom, or mop.

In many cities these workers lived in all or mostly black areas. In the largest cities, such as New York, Philadelphia, and Chicago, ghettos already had begun to emerge. But even where African Americans lived in racially mixed neighborhoods the trend was toward increased segregation. Blacks generally did not have access to housing elsewhere in the city, even if they earned enough to be more selective. Newcomers were immediately steered to districts known as "Little Africa" or the "Black Belt." African Americans who managed to circumvent efforts by real estate agents to keep blacks out of "white" areas were met with bombings or personal threats.

Black workers install a cobblestone street in a white residential neighborhood of Topeka, Kansas. Until World War I, African-American men living in cities were mainly relegated to jobs involving shovels, brooms, or other tools of manual labor. Few employers would hire them for factory work.

Black communities were diverse and included small business and professional classes. The middle class also included certain service workers. In Chicago, one of the most important judges of social standing in the black community was Julius Avendorph, whose job as personal assistant to businessman George Pullman entailed duties generally performed by a valet or a messenger. Only slightly further down the ladder stood the Pullman porters, men who worked the railroad sleeping and dining cars operated by Pullman's company. Their high status resulted in part from their relatively high job security and because many of them had high school—and in some cases even college—education.

Unlike their white counterparts, however, the black middle class—and even the minuscule black upper class—could not take advantage of the new housing available along transportation lines emerging from the city center. In a period when American cities were becoming increasingly segregated by class, African Americans remained residentially segregated by race instead.

RIVERSIDE
THE HOME OF BETTER PICTURES

Smoke
MO
TOBA

NO OTHER
TOBACCO
IS LIKE IT

Camels
SLOWER-BURNING
COSTLIER TOBACCOS

LUMBERTON TOBACCO MARKET

CAROLINA | WED. 15
THEATRE LUMBERTON | AUG.
IN PERSON
FRED KIRBY
THE VICTORY COWBOY
SINGING and YODELING "STAR" OF THE FAMOUS WBT
BRIARHOPPERS
FEATURING HIS
Nationally Known RADIO STARS
DIRECT FROM
C.B.S. COAST to COAST
CAROLINA HAYRIDE
Also THE CHAMPIONS OF HARMONY
THE CAROLINA PLAYBOYS
Carl McABEE — Ralph DAVIS
Blacky BOLYNN — Little "PEE WEE"

COLORED   WHITE

CHAPTER 2

THE "WHITE PROBLEM"
◇ ◇ ◇

James Weldon Johnson remembered well his introduction to the full implications of what it meant to be a black man in the United States. As a student at Atlanta University in the 1890s he recognized that "education for me meant, fundamentally, preparation to meet the tasks and exigencies of life as a Negro, a realization of the peculiar responsibilities due to my own racial group, and a comprehension of the application of American democracy to Negro citizens." The future songwriter, diplomat, writer, and civil rights leader did not learn this in the classroom; rather, he learned it on campus and around town. "Nearly all that was acquired, mental and moral," he recalled, "was destined to be fitted into a particular system of which 'race' was the center."

Johnson, of course, already knew that he was "a Negro," and that race mattered. He had grown up in Jacksonville, Florida, after the overthrow of Reconstruction. Although his family was better off than most African Americans (his father was a headwaiter at a hotel, his mother, a teacher), they experienced the same exclusions, acts of discrimination, and affronts to their dignity that other black Southerners suffered as white Southerners began to reestablish white supremacy.

Other African Americans at the turn of the century offer even more poignant turning points of social awareness. "I was a Negro come of age," Ellen Tarry later recalled, referring to her reaction the first time she saw a white person mercilessly beat a black Southerner for stepping out of his "place." Lyman Johnson, who grew up around the same time in a small Tennessee town, recalled that his "eyes were opened" when at age 14 he went inside the white school for the first time and saw the gymnasium.

The drinking fountains for Colored and White people were clearly marked throughout the South.

Looking at "that highly polished hardwood floor . . . in perfect amaze-
ment," Johnson later declared this as the moment he "found out how truly
unequal the Negro and white schools were."

Ellen Tarry, born in 1906 and later a schoolteacher, summed it up: "It
was the white man's world and I was not white." She and the two Johnsons
were learning their place in a social and economic system. At the same
time, however, their families and communities were teaching them how to
occupy that place with dignity. They learned how to perform roles without
accepting either the system or their place in it as natural, just, or inevitable.

These are Southern stories, but in the North things were not entirely
different; they simply carried a different twist. The most famous of such
recollections is that of W. E. B. Du Bois, describing a social snub he received
in the 1860s in Great Barrington, Massachusetts, at the tender age of six:

> Something put it into the boys' and girls' heads to buy gorgeous
> visiting–cards—ten cents a package—and exchange. The exchange was
> merry, till one girl, a tall newcomer, refused my card,—refused it peremp-
> torily, with a glance. Then it dawned on me with a certain suddenness that I
> was different from the others; or like, mayhap, in heart and life and longing,
> but shut out from their world by a vast veil.

All of these people had already experienced racism. But a striking
moment, a sudden burst of recognition, permitted them to dramatize a
fundamental fact of growing up as an African American. One had to learn
where the color line was, what it meant, how and when to cross it, and
how to maintain one's self-respect when it could not be crossed. To these
individuals and thousands of other African Americans who would spend
a good part of their lives trying to destroy that line, that moment was
the beginning of the rest of their life. They now entered the community's
debates about how best to struggle against formal and informal systems
of racial oppression.

The 20th century opened on a South that was busy constructing a
legal system that defined African Americans as something less than second-
class citizens. From the collapse of Reconstruction in the 1870s until the
1890s, black Southerners had been informally segregated or excluded out-
right from most social services and many public places. Provision for black
public schools was minimal, even in cities. Yet black Southerners still could
vote, and occasionally held the balance of power in a local election. Despite white control of all major institutions, white supremacy had not yet
been written into the law.

A variety of forces combined during the 1890s to prompt white Southerners to establish explicitly and concretely the place of black people in Southern society and politics. The threat posed by a potential alliance between black and white small farmers certainly played a part. Equally important, however, was a perception among whites that young black men and women were growing increasingly troublesome, in contrast to the older generation of blacks, who whites viewed as more docile.

During the late 1880s and early 1890s, black and white farmers had begun to form political coalitions based on their common status as renters or owners of small farms. Although the main organizer of small farmers, the Southern Farmers' Alliance, excluded African Americans, it did support the growth of a parallel organization, the Colored Farmers' National Alliance. The "Colored Alliance" reached its height in 1890, with a membership that probably hovered in the range of 250,000—an impressive accomplishment given the difficulty of organizing black farmers in an environment so hostile that meetings had to be conducted in secret.

This black-owned cotton gin in Madison County, Alabama, was a rare example of African-American involvement in the commercial aspects of the cotton economy. Like most of the land itself, the businesses that marketed the cotton were owned by whites.

The Farmers' Alliance movement (including the Colored Alliance) advanced in the 1890s from winning local elections to organizing a third political party. This party, the Populist party, posed a revolutionary challenge to Southern political and economic leaders because of its potential for an appeal to black and white small farmers based not on race but economic and social conditions.

A different kind of threat to social order was less tangible. By the 1890s a new generation of African Americans was reaching adulthood. These young men and women had never experienced slavery. They had experienced the violent overthrow of Reconstruction only as children. Unaccustomed to timidity toward whites and without vivid memories of the disillusion and despair following Reconstruction, they did not readily settle in places defined by the racial etiquette that had emerged during the previous two decades. This was especially true in cities and towns, where black populations were increasing despite the lack of regular employment for black men.

In an era when white Southerners were writing, reading, and reminiscing about a mythical antebellum South characterized by harmony between the races brought by slavery, these seemingly rootless young African Americans could seem threatening indeed. "The negroes are being overbearing and need toning down," declared one Louisiana newspaper in 1896.

Most white Southerners continued to believe that the descendants of Africans remained at a lower stage of civilization than Europeans and their descendants. In the early 20th century, Southern historian Ulrich B. Phillips would describe the slave plantation as a school, and most white Southerners were certain that emancipation had freed a people who had been dismissed from the school of slavery too early. White Southerners, observed a Northern white journalist traveling through Atlanta, "want the new South, but the Old Negro." Black people who did not know their place, did not acknowledge their subordinate status, and did not recognize the folly of trying to reach too high were considered dangerous.

This notion of "place" was central to the role of African Americans in Southern life. Place referred partly to where "the Negro" could fit in the Southern economy: mainly in agriculture. Blacks were to grow the cotton. Jobs in the industries processing the cotton into cloth were generally reserved for whites. Where the "Negro's place" was not agricultural, it was servile. Whites gave orders; blacks did their bidding.

Few whites reflected on the justice of this pattern. Most assumed it was simply natural, a result of each race's aptitudes. Mississippi planter Alfred Holt Stone proclaimed confidently in 1908, "Speaking of the average [Negroes], their actions have no logical or reasonable basis, . . . they are notional and whimsical, and . . . they are controlled far more by their fancies than by their common sense."

Place also referred to the location of African Americans in Southern culture, a subordinate role that was enacted and reenacted on the street, in the store, and elsewhere in the daily lives of Southerners. By the turn of the century, black men had learned to doff their hat, to step into the street at the approach of a white person, to speak deferentially. Black men were never "Mister," black women never "Miss" or "Missus." Even those black Southerners who had managed to move into the business or professional ranks were reminded of the limited nature of their accomplishment. They might have escaped the working class, but they could never escape the burden of race. As one white boy told Lyman Johnson's father, a principal at

During cotton picking season in the fall, black Southerners could always find work dragging a sack down the seemingly endless rows of cotton bolls.

the black school in Columbia, Tennessee, "I don't care how educated you Johnsons are. . . . I don't care what kind of jobs you got. You're all niggers."

Yet to most white Southerners, it mattered very much how educated "their negroes" were, and what kinds of jobs they had. "What I want here is negroes who can make cotton," declared the owner of a plantation in the Mississippi Delta, "and they don't need education to help them make cotton." An education, declared one of his neighbors, would only provide a Negro with an ambition "to get out of his place."

Low-wage labor that could be easily coerced was central to the Southern economy. The inheritance of the plantation economy, coupled with prevailing ideas about race, contributed to the development of a legal system that left blacks peculiarly vulnerable to domination by their employers and landlords. "What could we do?" declared a black Georgian forced to work without pay to settle a fraudulent debt. "The white folks had all the courts, all the guns, all the hounds, all the railroads, all the telegraph wires, all the newspapers, all the money, and nearly all the land."

A white attorney in Mississippi explained in 1914 (six years before taking office as a judge) that "an important branch of the law here in Mississippi" was "Negro law." This law was unwritten, and at its center was the premise of African-American powerlessness.

Given how easy it was for white landlords and employers to call the shots they considered it essential that African Americans remain in the South at the bottom of the heap—available for work that nobody else would do. Any education black Southerners received should not, as one Southern governor put it, give them aspirations "beyond the sphere of negro life." The general consensus in Mississippi at the turn of the century was that "the negro must be kept ignorant and destitute in order to manage him safely."

African Americans who did prosper in the South around the turn of the century learned not to flaunt that success in front of whites. "I know men who won't keep a horse," remarked an Alabama man in 1912. "If they get one they will sell it. If you ask such a one why he sold his horse, he'd very likely say: 'A white man see me 'n dat 'ere horse, he look hard at me.'"

A joke that made the rounds of Southern black communities described the absurdity of this hostility to the fruits of hard work in a country that had put hard work and prosperity at the center of its national creed. A white Southern man leaving a railroad station with a white visitor from the North notices two black men, one fast asleep and the other engrossed in a newspaper. He kicks the man who is reading. The Northerner, taken aback, asks his host why he would kick the "industrious Negro." Why not kick the lazy man out of his slumber? "He's not the one we're worried about," replies the Southerner.

This concern with blacks not accepting their place reveals a lasting tension within Southern white culture. On the one hand, early-20th-century white Southerners tended to be confident that their black workers, tenants, and servants were "amiable." As one Southern railroad manager explained, referring to the place of African Americans in his work force, "We find them especially amiable, docile, and obedient. . . . There is no better labor among any race in the world." Many whites in the ruling elite agreed that "the Negro" accepted "the place assigned him by the white man." African Americans thus constituted the perfect labor force: easily coerced, unlikely to organize, and readily available because they supposedly lacked the ambition and aptitude to do anything else.

Existing side by side with this confidence, however, was a set of fears. Those whites who saw blacks as a race teetering on the edge of barbarism worried about the aggressions lurking beneath the thin veneer of amiability. Moreover, white Southerners either remembered Reconstruction or had grown up hearing the recollections of their parents—recollections enveloped in myths of evil white Northerners bent on revenge and profit and allied with illiterate black legislators intent on legalizing racial intermarriage.

These memories were furthered poisoned by the myths of corruption and incompetence that hid the accomplishments of the relatively rational, clean, and progressive state governments of the Reconstruction period. But they also included accurate images of black men voting, carrying guns, and taking their landlords to court. The danger of black political participation was clear to white Southerners who wished to learn from history rather than repeat it.

White Southerners had perfectly good reason to fear that African Americans did not accept things the way they were. Black men were moving around more, finding employment in the expanding seasonal turpentine and lumber industries. Less tied to the land than their parents, young African Americans were increasingly moving to the city, especially after the depression of the 1890s sent cotton prices cascading downward. Women were welcomed as domestics but men had no settled place in the urban economy. Strikes by black domestic workers, longshoremen, lumber workers, and railroad men were unusual events, but point to an increased unwillingness among black workers to accept their place.

Black men and women were also determined to become educated. It made no difference to them that white Southerners feared that an educated Negro would not know his "place." One Tennessee schoolteacher explained to his son the relationship between education and resisting white notions of where blacks fit in Southern life. Without an education, he explained, "you're always at the beck and call of white people." Between 1870 and 1910, the literacy rate among black Southerners increased from 19 percent to 61 percent.

By the last decade of the 19th century, many white Southerners were growing increasingly concerned that their black neighbors, employees, servants, and tenants would not accept their place. It seemed that protocol and custom no longer held behavior in check. Even intimidation required more effort.

In cities reports of blacks resisting arrest had been on the rise since the late 1880s. Complaining of black servants referring to one another as "Miss Johnson" or "Mr. Jones," one Louisiana newspaper identified the nub of the issue: "The younger generation of negro bucks and wenches have lost that wholesome respect for the white man, without which two races, the one inferior, cannot live in peace and harmony together."

To some white Southerners the answer to this apparent threat to white supremacy lay in increased levels of intimidation. The result was an epidemic of lynching in the South, beginning in 1882 and rising to a peak a decade later. Seeking retribution or revenge on behalf of a community, lynch mobs acted outside the legal system despite their claim to represent the interest of law and order.

These acts of violence—which usually resulted in either death or severe injury to the victim—were not unique to the South. During the American Revolution lynch mobs singled out individuals suspected of loyalty to the English crown. Nineteenth-century American lynch mobs assumed the right to maintain order in frontier communities and attacked men and women who advocated such unpopular causes as antislavery. But by the end of the 19th century, other than occasional labor organizers, African Americans were the major target of Americans who sought to defend community values and order through collective violence against helpless individuals.

What set the South apart was the central role of race in this pattern of terrorism. More than 2,000 black Southerners were killed by white mobs

It was not unusual for white Southerners to lynch black citizens accused of crimes before they could be tried in a court. The whites were proud of their actions and often happy to be photographed with their victims.

between 1884 and 1900. The victims tended to be men who had violated place in one of two ways: by becoming too big for the tight-fitting britches of white supremacy, or by breaking loose from ties to a community in which they were "known" and then committing some minor transgression elsewhere. Men could be lynched for anything "from violating labor contracts to 'shooting rabbits,'" observed Ida B. Wells, the editor of *Free Speech,* a Memphis newspaper.

White Southerners, even those who disapproved of lynching, defended the practice as necessary to protect virtuous white womanhood from oversexed and uncontrolled black men. That was an "old threadbare lie," declared Wells in 1892. Northerners who kept hearing that lie would eventually come to different conclusions about Southerners, suggested Wells, conclusions that would "be very damaging to the moral reputation of their women."

Fortunately for Wells, she was in New York when her sentiments were published in a Philadelphia newspaper. The Memphis press revealed the limits of free speech in the South by calling for a lynching. "There are some things that the Southern white man will not tolerate," declared one white newspaper. Unable to destroy Wells herself, a crowd that included leading white citizens of the city destroyed her printing presses.

In the 1890s, Wells would publish two statistical analyses of lynching, revealing that her narrow escape was atypical only in that most victims were men. Lynching was not the work of rabble; men of property and standing were also involved. Furthermore, less than one lynching in five involved even an accusation of rape. Nor was lynching a response to threats

At the peak of its power in the 1920s, the Ku Klux Klan marches down Pennsylvania Avenue in Washington, D.C., in 1926. Its members hid behind masks and robes as they terrorized black citizens. Catholics and Jews also attracted Klan hatred during the 1920s.

to white womanhood. The Southern rape fantasy, Wells declared, was "an excuse to get rid of Negroes who were acquiring wealth and property and thus keep the race terrorized." Lynching was not done for the sake of terror itself, or out of loyalty to an idea, but to maintain order as white Southerners knew it.

But this was a disorderly way to go about maintaining order. Southern white elites—men who published newspapers, owned plantations, sat on the boards of banks and railroads, and pulled strings behind the scenes in the Democratic party—recognized that violence outside the legal system undermined the majesty of the law. Politically, however, it was unwise to condemn lynching more forcefully than a gentle chiding after each grisly murder of an African American. Lynchings, after all, were community events, festivals that parents attended with small children, holding them high in the air to afford a better view of the victim twisting in a noose or burning at the stake.

Lynchings were not only disorderly. They also gave the region a bad press in the North. This was the early heyday of "yellow journalism," a new kind of newspaper publishing that attracted readers by appealing largely to their emotions. Lurid tales of Southern violence provided good copy, especially when tinged either with accusations of sexual violence or with a crowd's determination to cut off a victim's sexual organs. White Northerners, drawing on a long tradition of satisfying their consciences by expressing sympathy to black victims of Southern racism, seized on vivid descriptions of lynchings as continued evidence of Southern backwardness.

These twin threats posed by lynching—disregard for legal procedures and the possibility of federal intervention generated by outrage from the North—roused the Southern white establishment. White disorder had to be curbed, a task that required eliminating the instability and uncertainty in race relations that underlay that disorder. Blacks had to be kept in their place by other means. Across the South, state constitutions, state legislation, and city ordinances were rewritten to enshrine in law the subordinate place of black people in Southern life. Black male Southerners would no longer vote or serve on juries. Separation of the races would be required by law.

First, African Americans were eliminated from the political system. Although black voting had already declined by 1890 as a result of white terrorism and ballot-box fraud, new legislation ensured that black men could not tip the balance of power between white contenders for office.

Mob violence would no longer be necessary to maintain the political system as a white preserve. The methods were, by necessity, ingenious, because they had to skirt the 15th Amendment to the United States Constitution, which stated, "The right of citizens of the United States to vote shall not be denied or abridged by the United States or by any State on account of race, color, or previous condition of servitude."

How then to disfranchise blacks? The answer lay in broad barriers to participation, with loopholes through which otherwise disqualified whites could squeeze. Poll taxes made it difficult for poor people to vote by requiring each voter to pay a few dollars for the privilege of casting a ballot. Property and literacy qualifications established additional barriers.

To induce understandably skeptical white workers and farmers to support such legislation, Southern white elites reminded them that white supremacy assured that black workers would never compete effectively for white men's jobs. These elites, the bankers, lawyers, plantation owners, publishers, and business owners in the South, also invoked inaccurate but widely believed images of Reconstruction as a Dark Age of corrupt and tyrannical black rule. Newspapers across the South reminded readers that although blacks had been shoved back in their place after Reconstruction they remained dangerous. Newspapers and politicians dramatized crimes committed by blacks, especially alleged rapes. The message was clear: whites had to stick together to protect their livelihoods, families, and way of life.

To reassure white voters that the goal was to disqualify only blacks, the legislation that set limits on voting established thinly concealed exceptions to the voting restrictions. Exempted were men determined by the (invariably white) registrar of voters to be of "good character" and men who could provide a reasonable explanation (in the judgment of the registrar) of a provision of the state constitution chosen by the registrar.

Also exempt were the direct descendants of men who had voted before Reconstruction—that is, the descendants of whites. Known as the "grandfather clause," this loophole was declared unconstitutional in 1915 by the United States Supreme Court in the case *Guinn* v. *United States*.

The "white primary" was a particularly effective way to limit black participation in voting. As an internal party mechanism it lay outside the poll tax requirements and could be limited to white voters by party rules. With the Republican party so weak as to be irrelevant, a victory in the Democratic primary was tantamount to election. Because primaries were "private" contests to determine the standard-bearers of a political party, rather than a general election, the courts did not declare the ruse in violation of constitutional guarantees.

The new measures were effective. In Mississippi, the president of the 1890 constitutional convention straightforwardly declared that "we came here to exclude the Negro," and the delegates did their job. Only black men who were economically independent or regarded by whites as "good" or "safe" Negroes remained on the voter rolls. By the turn of the century, only 10 percent of black men in Mississippi were registered to vote. Forty years later that proportion had dwindled to 0.4 percent (2,000 registered voters out of approximately 500,000 possible voters). Among Alabama's 181,471 African American men of voting age in 1900, only 3,000 were registered to vote. Across the South, the proportions were similar, and black voting remained insignificant until the 1960s.

Disfranchisement, or the stripping of people's right to vote, was an attack not only on black political influence—of which there was precious little by the turn of the century—but also on black manhood. Nineteenth-century Americans tied manhood and citizenship closely together. Both hinged on independence. Cast as naturally docile, unable to control their sexual passions, and economically dependent, black men were labeled as unfit for citizenship. Denying them the ballot reinforced their exclusion from the civic community.

Although the Supreme Court struck down the grandfather clause in 1915, Jim Crow and barriers to blacks' ability to vote remained in place.

The logical next step was to minimize disorder by minimizing contact between the races. Between 1890 and 1915, legislators across the South, as far west as Texas and Oklahoma, enacted a body of legislation known as the Jim Crow laws. This legislation ensured that however interdependent the races might be in the South, they would not inhabit the same public spaces. In the most ordinary and yet meaningful way African Americans in the South would constantly be reminded—especially in cities and towns—that they were people without social honor, people whose dignity had no official existence, people who were not a part of mainstream society.

In most cases the trains and railroad stations were the first targets of Jim Crow laws. One waiting room was marked "colored," the other "white." Next, rules of conduct were passed for streetcars—whites were seated from front to back, blacks from back to front. Some streetcar companies consid-

Jim Crow was alive and well in Southern railroad stations in the 1920s.

ered this a foolish business practice, expensive and needlessly antagonizing their large black clientele. But the laws required segregation. For the races to sit alongside each other was to imply equality; front to back versus back to front reminded one and all who belonged in front and who belonged in the back.

The legislation quickly extended to nearly all aspects of public life. Anything worth doing or building outside people's homes was worth a segregation ordinance: hotels, restaurants, restrooms, drinking fountains, parks, schools, libraries, saloons, telephone booths, theaters, doorways, stairways, prisons, cemeteries, and brothels. In some communities the ordinances even specified the size of the ubiquitous "whites only" or "colored" signs. Florida required separate storage facilities for school textbooks. In Georgia, courtrooms had two Bibles for swearing in witnesses.

This obsession with race, which reached its apex in the first decade of the 20th century, was not unique to the South. Throughout the United

States, the concept of race had become an increasingly important way of categorizing people and cultures. World atlases published during this period were less interested in economies or social systems than in the particular races inhabiting one place or another. Relying on the dominant theories in the social and physical sciences, powerful decision-makers in government and industry divided the American population into a staggering array of "races." Armenians, Gypsies, Ruthenians, Jews, Syrians, Greeks, Italians, Africans: each was a separate race, each with its own characteristics.

Northern industrialists devised hiring policies reminiscent of 18th-century Southern slaveholders who had been certain that Africans from one area made better slaves than men and women from another part of the continent. Thus Poles and Slavs were presumed to be suited to tasks requiring great physical exertion; Jews, Italians, and Portuguese supposedly had an aptitude for lighter, repetitive tasks that required a keen eye or nimble finger. Italians were unstable and untidy "but not destructive," noted one Milwaukee industrialist, who lamented that they drank too much (though less than the Greeks), quarreled, and did not understand modern machinery. Hungarians, although "thrifty and honest" in the view of another employer, were not clean. In most variations of this complex scheme, "Africans" were considered inefficient, incapable of mechanical labor, emotional rather than rational, oversexed, and in general a cut below everyone else.

The South differed from the rest of the country in the relative simplicity of its racial roster. There race remained largely a question of black and white. White Northerners and Westerners, although equally inclined to think in racial terms, were less likely than their Southern counterparts to translate those ideas into a system of rigid distinctions embodied in the law. They shared white Southerners' assumptions about the capabilities of the descendants of Africans, but the diversity of the population in these regions complicated the equation.

Greenwood, Mississippi, maintained a separate public library for its black residents.

In the West, "Asiatic races," especially the Chinese, seemed a more threatening presence than the small black population. There was, of course, considerable variation. James Weldon Johnson, a performer traveling with his brother in 1905, could secure no hotel accommodations in Salt Lake City. They had considerable difficulty even finding a place to eat. A few days later in San Francisco they easily secured a room and dined without incident. Yet even in San Francisco patterns were uneven. The manager of a leading hotel there explained at the turn of the century that incidents seldom occurred, largely because "the colored people who travel . . . do not often place themselves or us in embarrassing positions."

In the North, race was complicated by the multiplicity of European nationalities. Blacks were not essential to the labor market. Their ability to vote generally aroused little concern because their numbers were relatively small until the 1920s. Few whites considered their presence a threat to social stability. This would begin to change in the 1920s, as social theories increasingly reduced "race" to a triad of black/white/yellow (with American Indians either a fourth race or thrown in as descendants of Asians), and as a growing black population came to play a major role in urban culture and politics. Until World War I, however, "race" as a division between two groups was largely a Southern way of thinking.

Because most Southern states by the first decade of the century had passed laws governing race and social interaction from marriage to public transportation to circus entrances and exits, it was essential to create usable definitions. How did one decide who was "a Negro"? Skin tones, after all, could suggest only so much in a society in which Africans, Europeans, and Indians—none of whom were uniformly tinted to begin with—had mingled over the centuries.

In New Orleans, for example, the population was considerably more diverse than elsewhere in the South. Because of a long history of sexual relations between people of European and African descent, skin hues ranged infinitely. A streetcar official explained why the new segregation law required clear, if arbitrary, definitions: "Our conductors are men of intelligence, but the greatest ethnologist the world ever saw would be at a loss to classify streetcar passengers in this city."

Apparently the only possible solution was to "eyeball" passengers and rely on conventional assumptions about the physical characteristics that distinguished "black" from "white." Indeed, this was the approach of the United States Bureau of the Census, which instructed its enumerators until

1920 to categorize an individual by estimating the proportion of African blood according to color and other features.

This might work for the census, but racially segregated institutions needed more exact ways of determining inclusion and exclusion. The color line had to be defined to regulate such important civic activities as school enrollments, marriage, and jury service. A question with serious social implications everywhere in the United States also had wide-ranging legal implications in the South.

Southern states divided roughly equally in how their laws defined race. Approximately half defined "a Negro" as anyone with "a trace of black ancestry." Nearly all the rest identified anyone with at least one-eighth "Negro blood" (one great-grandparent) as "colored." Yet this solution to the problem of categorization was neither inevitable nor "natural." Why should a child with one parent of European descent and one parent of African descent be a "Negro"? How much genealogical research was to be required to define someone's legal status?

Elsewhere in the Western hemisphere, societies used a broad variety of categories. Even in the United States the terms *mulatto* (half and half), *quadroon* (three white grandparents, one black) and *octoroon* (one black grandparent, seven white) were frequently used, both in popular speech and even (at least in the case of "mulatto") in the United States Census until 1920. Indeed, the decision to drop "mulatto" as a category that year resulted from bureau estimates that 75 percent of all African Americans were of "mixed blood," and eyeballing the difference between "Negroes" and "mulattoes" was impossible. Anyway, the only categories that mattered were those required by the Southern laws. "One drop" of Negro blood sullied the purity of whiteness, pushing an individual across the color line.

The legal existence and meaning of these categories was ratified by the United States Supreme Court in 1896. In the case of *Plessy* v. *Ferguson,* the court ruled that state laws requiring racially segregated facilities were permissible under the Constitution as long as the facilities were "equal." They never were. But it would take nearly 60 years for American law to recognize that inequality. Not until 1954 would the Supreme Court begin dismantling Jim Crow by ruling in *Brown* v. *Board of Education* that "separate educational facilities are inherently unequal."

African Americans, of course, understood the relationship between segregation and inequality from the beginning. In the North and West the patterns of segregation were less formalized and less complete. Schools

The black schools of the South offered minimal education, often for only a few months a year. One former student recalled, "You could barely learn the alphabet in three months."

generally were not segregated because black communities either were too small or insufficiently concentrated to create separate districts. Nevertheless, black children were treated differently by teachers who assumed they were less capable than their white peers.

In most Northern states discrimination in public places was prohibited by law. Restaurant staff were instructed to treat black customers rudely, to ignore them, or to lace their food with such massive quantities of salt as to render it inedible. There were no laws against employment discrimination; it was widespread. In a nation where European immigrants became "white" as part of the Americanization process, racial distinctions were deeply embedded in language, habits of interaction, social and political institutions, and countless other aspects of everyday life.

ST. JOHN A.M.E. CHURCH

SUNDAY

J. S. JACKSON, PASTOR

TENTH ANNIVER
N.A.A
CLEVELAND, OHIO

CHAPTER 3

BUILDING COMMUNITIES

T he Independent Order of St. Luke was in trouble. Founded in Maryland in 1867 to provide sickness and death benefits to dues-paying members, the order had flourished for two decades, rapidly expanding to New York and Virginia. But in 1899, in part because of the deepest economic depression the nation had yet experienced, the organization was virtually bankrupt. After 30 years in office its chief executive resigned, leaving his successor $31.61 in cash and $400 in debts.

The new Grand Worthy Secretary, Maggie Lena Walker, assumed her position at a fraction of her predecessor's salary. Under her leadership the Order of St. Luke not only survived but flourished. From 57 councils with 1,080 members, it grew to 2,020 councils which enrolled more than 100,000 members in 28 states. Guided by Walker's commitment to expanding economic opportunities for African Americans, the order established programs for black youth, an educational loan fund, a weekly newspaper, a department store, and a bank. Walker and her colleagues in St. Luke led a boycott against segregated streetcars in Richmond, Virginia, in 1904. The *St. Luke Herald,* the organization's paper, took positions opposing segregation, lynching, and discrimination against black job seekers.

Maggie Lena Walker was the first woman in the United States to serve as president of a bank. Born in Richmond, Virginia, in 1867, Walker graduated from that city's Colored Normal School (a teachers' college) 16 years later. By then she already had shared the work experience of most urban African-American women, helping her widowed mother with child care and with the laundry taken in to make ends meet. Her degree qualified her to teach in Richmond's segregated black schools, but she was forced to resign when she married.

The NAACP held its 10th anniversary convention in Cleveland, Ohio, in 1919. Among the issues that the delegates considered were race riots that followed the return of black soldiers from World War I.

Walker had joined the Independent Order of St. Luke when she was 14 and by 1899 had held numerous leadership positions in the organization. During the next three decades she would supplement her leadership of the Order of St. Luke with active involvement in the woman suffrage movement, Richmond Council of Colored Women, Virginia State Federation of Colored Women, National Association of Wage Earners, International Council of Women of the Darker Races, National Training School for Girls, Richmond Urban League, and the National Association for the Advancement of Colored People.

Maggie Lena Walker: banker, teacher, reformer, activist, laundress, suffragist, executive.

Maggie Lena Walker's career suggests both the challenges faced by African-American communities in the early 20th century and the diversity of initiatives fashioned by black leadership to meet those challenges. Although she was speaking of women in particular, Walker effectively described where African Americans as a group stood and where they had to go: "To avoid the traps and snares of life," they would have to "band themselves together, organize . . . put their mites together, put their hands and their brains together and make work and business for themselves."

Walker was calling for what her biographer has termed a "community of struggle." This community could be diverse, encompassing men, women, and children; businesspeople and domestic servants; preachers and sinners. It also could accommodate differences of opinion. But to be a community capable of moving forward it would have to encompass a people aware of their common past and shared future. The long agenda suggested by Walker's career meant that no single approach, no focus on any single organization, could define African-American leadership or purpose.

For African Americans in the early 20th century this struggle had two related and mutually supportive components. One was to build community institutions such as schools, churches, businesses, clubs, and lodges within the African-American world. The other was to fight for integration into American institutional life, to integrate schools, workplaces, residential neighborhoods, public accommodations like hotels and restaurants, and especially councils of government. Even today these goals are often presented as alternatives, warring strategies competing for the loyalty of people forced to choose one path or the other.

Presenting these alternatives as a harsh choice is misleading. Although particular leaders and institutions did express competing visions and emphases, activism took place simultaneously at many levels. When

An African-American dental office in 1926.

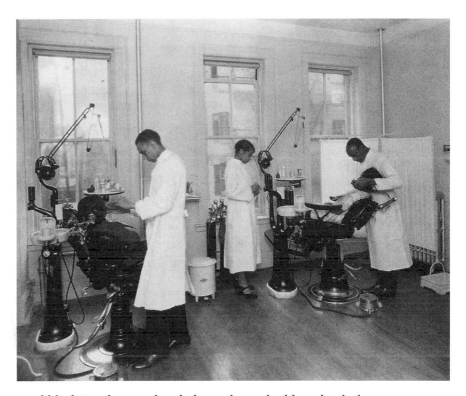

rural black Southerners banded together to build a school, they were engaging in self-help while at the same time yielding to segregation. But they also were resisting white assumptions about the appropriate form of education for their children. They were insisting on a literacy that defied Southern white definitions of their "place." To build a school was to participate in the struggle for equality.

Yet the quest for integration did not always reflect a desire to mix with white people. Despite the ruling of the U.S. Supreme Court in *Plessy* v. *Ferguson* that separate institutions were constitutional only if they were equal, African Americans recognized that in practice separate always meant unequal. Thus blacks frequently fought for integration into white institutions in order to gain access to better services or commodities. By living among whites, a Los Angeles journalist observed, black Californians could secure "the best fire, water, and police protection."

Robert and Mary Church Terrell made the same judgment in Washington, D.C. The first president of the National Association of Colored Women, Mary Terrell was one of the most prominent women in the United States. Robert Terrell was an attorney and eventually a federal

At camp meetings, church members gathered for intensive sessions of prayer, preaching, and songs. Many preachers had little formal training, and tended to conduct services that were highly emotional.

judge. They did not necessarily want to live among white neighbors, she later recalled of their search for a house. But housing in "white" neighborhoods was "more modern" (in other words, better equipped and in better condition). It also was less expensive. Real estate agents selling homes in "Negro" neighborhoods could price properties higher because African Americans had access to only a small portion of the city's housing market. For the Terrells and others, the struggle for integration did reflect sentiment for increased contact across the color line. But even many integrationists were wary of whites, seeking integration only because the color line divided the powerful from the powerless.

Whether building community institutions or battering the walls of racial separation and discrimination, African Americans had to mobilize limited resources. These resources included a long history—dating from slavery—of community life built on families and religion. In the rural South the other major institution to emerge after emancipation was the school. In towns and cities these institutions joined with women's clubs, fraternal societies, businesses, and social service organizations to shape African-American community life and provide the basis for activism.

Other than the family, the oldest African-American institution was the church. "Free Negroes" in cities had created their own congregations as early as the 18th century. Building on independent religious traditions among slaves, the number of these Baptist and Methodist churches grew rapidly after emancipation.

African-American styles of religious worship remained an aspect of a

A black minister baptizes three women in the Ohio River. Clergymen were highly respected leaders within African-American communities.

distinctive African-American culture. Although African-American religious practices varied widely, depending on class, denomination, and region, the dominant currents arose in the rural South, where vivid preaching and dramatic conversion experiences played a central role. Except in the more sedate churches of the urban middle class (especially in the North), services tended to be interactive, with the congregation responding verbally during the sermon and the minister taking cues from those responses.

In addition the church as an institution and a physical structure provided a space beyond the gaze of whites. This was especially important in the South during and immediately after Reconstruction. Black churches occupied a space beyond white interference. There African Americans could organize, debate, and promote educational activities. The Sunday service itself could provide a welcome respite from a week of backbreaking toil and the anxieties of dealing with white folks.

By the beginning of the 20th century the church brought together African Americans as no other institution possibly could. In 1906 more than half of the nearly 7 million African Americans 10 years or older belonged to churches, a proportion comparable to patterns among white Americans. Much more striking is the number of African Americans united in a few particular organizations. The National Baptist Convention, the largest black institution in the United States, claimed more than 2.2 million members. The African Methodist Episcopal (A.M.E.) church constituted the second largest denomination, with nearly 500,000 members.

Like most white Southerners, African-American Christians tended to be fundamentalists, men and women who read their Bibles literally and worshiped energetically. Especially in the rural South and in working-class urban churches, black Americans demanded that their ministers evoke emotional responses with powerful sermons. A pastor's ability to "shout" his congregation (to arouse a vocal expression of passion during the sermon) measured his leadership as well as his spiritual credentials.

The greatest heights of ecstasy were often reached in Holiness and Pentecostal churches, which emphasized the importance of a worshipper's personal experience with the Holy Spirit. At first attracting both black and white Southerners, Holiness and Pentecostal sects grew most rapidly after 1910. Subsequently, as Southerners moved north and west these sects expanded, especially into the urban Midwest.

African-American churches were not, however, merely places where people went for relief from the burdens of everyday life. "The social life of the Negro centres in his church," W. E. B. Du Bois observed in his 1899 study, *The Philadelphia Negro*. "Baptism, wedding and burial, gossip and courtship, friendship and intrigue—all lie within these walls." Many ministers and deacons (lay leaders) complemented their inspirational roles with political activity, or served as community spokesmen. In middle-class churches, where emotional behavior was rejected as "undecorous," a pastor might provide intellectual leadership as well.

In rural areas and small towns, churches often were the only gathering places available outside of small business establishments. People would

The International Religious Congress of Triumph, The Church, and Kingdom of God in Christ, held in Indianapolis in the summer of 1919, lasted for 50 days.

come together in the church to discuss building a school or respond to a threatened lynching. They would share information and opinions about migration to the new "black towns" being established in Oklahoma, to agricultural areas touted by labor agents, or to Northern cities.

Although Southern cities had other gathering places, churches still functioned as one of the most important community institutions. Social services and emergency support were especially common because so many black Southerners could secure only irregular employment. A strong sense of extended family helped, providing a network of support during periods of unemployment. Beyond the family lay the church, whose members gave freely when they could and received without shame when in need.

In Atlanta, most black churches took an "after collection" each Sunday, to be distributed to members in financial distress. Fifth Street Baptist in Louisville collected and distributed clothing, paid for funerals of members unable to afford proper burial, awarded an annual college scholarship, and held annual fundraising drives for an orphanage, a home for the elderly, and a local black college.

Northern churches were likely to add to this traditional form of charity with programs influenced by early-20th-century progressive reform movements. Under the leadership of Reverend Reverdy Ransom, the Institutional A.M.E. Church in Chicago resembled a settlement house, providing a wide variety of social services to the neighborhood. After finding a job through Institutional's employment bureau, a black worker could

leave her child at its kindergarten or day nursery. Classes in sewing, cooking, stenography, and typing taught useful skills. Leisure opportunities included concerts, lectures, a reading room, and a gymnasium.

More typical in its less ambitious program was Antioch Baptist Church in Cleveland, which sponsored boys' and girls' clubs, choral groups, and a recreation center located in two adjacent houses. Destitute members received cash assistance. North and South, black churches and denominational associations published newspapers, provided social welfare services, helped congregants find jobs, and provided recreational facilities.

These activities required time and money. In most black churches the greatest energy came from the volunteer labor of the women who raised money from communities that had little cash to spare. The role of women as church activists was particularly evident in the National Baptist Convention, where they constituted two-thirds of the membership. In 1906, 43 percent of all female African Americans who had reached their 10th birthday belonged to the National Baptist Convention. Men, however, dominated the organization's leadership, occupied the pulpits, and controlled the finances.

Just as African Americans in general looked to the church as an institution independent of white domination, black women determined that they needed an organization within the church that would provide them with a similar degree of independence. Founded in 1900, the Woman's Convention of the National Baptist Convention quickly grew to 1 million members, providing many women with their introduction to community activism.

This experience in local churches and in the Women's Convention brought many black women into the emerging women's club movement. Some nineteenth-century black women's clubs had been formed to aid particular institutions, especially orphanages and homes for the elderly and infirm. In many cities, African Americans established Phillis Wheatley Associations (named after the 18th-century black poet) to assist women arriving unaccompanied from the countryside.

Most common were the more socially inclined literary societies. These and church groups formed the backbone of the National Association of Colored Women (NACW), created in 1896. Yet the NACW also drew on the reform-oriented clubs, with the Boston Women's Era Club playing an especially important role. The founders of this club, Josephine St. Pierre Ruffin and her daughter, Florida Ruffin Ridley, created the first

Ninth Annual Conference ..

OF THE

Rhode Island Union

OF

| Colored Women's Clubs |

AT THE

Union Baptist Church
SCHOOL STREET
Pawtucket, R. I.

Thursday October 12, 1911

OFFICERS

President, Miss MARY E. JACKSON, Providence.
1st Vice-Pres. Mrs. H. R. NELSON, Newport
2nd Vice-Pres. Mrs. SUSAN WILLIAMS, Providence
3rd Vice-Pres. Mrs. C. BIRCHMORE, Pawtucket
General Secretary Miss JACINTHIA PERRY, Providence
Asst. Secretary, Miss GRACE STEPHENSON, Newport
Treasurer, Mrs. W. ALLISON, Pawtucket
Organizer, Mrs. W. WORTHEN, Providence.

Street Car Directions:---Going east along Main Street from either the Station of the Terminus of any of the Providence cars across the bridge leads direct to School Street.

Women's clubs varied from purely social gatherings to religious activities and social services.

monthly magazine published by African-American women, *Women's Era,* established in 1894 (the same year as the club). It had correspondents across the United States and reached thousands of readers. Its editors called for the 1895 conference that eventually became the NACW. The NACW grew quickly, from 5,000 members in the late 1890s to 50,000 in the 1910s and 100,000 a decade later.

Membership in the NACW came mainly from the urban elite—generally teachers and wives of professionals, ministers, and business-men. These women shared with their white peers a concern with upholding traditional standards of morality and respectability amid the turmoil of movement from country to city and changes in employment from farm to factory. And, like black men, they organized to challenge the increasing level of racism at the turn of the century.

But they carried a double burden, as African Americans and as women. *Outlook,* a Northern reform magazine, reflected commonplace white perceptions of black women: "The brain of a child and the passions of a woman, steeped in centuries of ignorance and savagery and wrapped about with immemorial vices." Taking as their motto "Lifting As We Climb," black clubwomen recognized that their destiny was inextricably intertwined with less-privileged African Americans. If they could elevate other black women to their standards of morality and manners, then the black masses would be lifted up from the gutter of poverty and degradation. At the same time they would win from white America the acceptance they deserved by dint of their middle-class values and position.

Although the NACW did achieve recognition as an affiliate of the largely white National Council of Women in 1901, black women generally encountered difficulties with major women's reform organizations at the turn of the century. As the suffrage, temperance (anti-liquor), and women's club movements moved toward national organization, they had to consider the sensibilities of white Southerners. Black women actively participated in local movements on behalf of woman suffrage and temperance in many Northern cities. But at the very moment that American feminism was moving more visibly onto a national stage, African-American women found themselves pushed to the margins.

The urge to participate in "white" clubs and in "white" feminist organizations did not necessarily signal a desire to turn away from the black community toward a largely white social environment. White women who worried that black women seeking to join their suffrage organizations or the Women's Christian Temperance Union sought "social equality" deluded themselves. Black women simply recognized that these larger, more broadly based organizations could provide stronger backing and more visible platforms.

Indeed, like other black institutions, black women's clubs and reform societies owed their existence only partly to exclusion from white institutions. Black communities faced problems different from those confronted by white reformers. Like their white counterparts, NACW affiliates sponsored kindergartens, day nurseries, training schools, orphanages, and clubs for mothers. But they did so in response to a community with unique needs and limited resources.

Black women's clubs represented a type of institution whose roots lay in African-American fraternal societies (lodges) and mutual benefit associations. The distinctions between the two kinds of voluntary organizations were not always clear. Generally lodges were places for recreation for their members, and membership in a lodge was considered a badge of social respectability. Mutual benefit associations, by contrast, were likely to focus more on insurance functions, especially death benefits.

By the end of the century, these organizations had increasing overlapping functions. Nearly all provided members with burial and life insurance. Some, like the Independent Order of St. Luke, which was unusual in that it included both men and women, operated small businesses or banks. Nearly all provided opportunities for leadership.

Membership in a fraternal order could provide African-American men with a badge of respectable manhood within the community. A black man denied civic recognition in the Jim Crow South was somebody when he wore the uniform of the Elks, Knights of Pythias, Masons, Oddfellows, or any one of a number of other lodges. The largest order was the Oddfellows, with more than 300,000 members by 1904. The famed jazz

*The King Tut Lodge
of the IBPOEW in
Cleveland. Member-
ship in lodges per-
mitted African
Americans to estab-
lish important busi-
ness, social, and
political connections.*

musician Louis Armstrong recalled the importance of the lodge when he
was a boy in New Orleans:

> Dad was a sharp man, tall and handsome and well built. He made the
> chicks swoon when he marched by as the grand marshal in the Odd
> Fellows parade. I was very proud to see him in his uniform and his high
> hat with the beautiful streamer hanging down by his side. Yes, he was a
> fine figure of a man, my dad. Or at least that is the way he seemed to me
> as a kid when he strutted by like a peacock at the head of the Odd
> Fellows parade.

North and South, fraternal (men's) and sororital (women's) organizations were an integral aspect of urban culture among the mass of working-
class black men and women. In the North, lodge membership provided
men with political connections and stature. Robert R. Jackson, who was
elected to the Illinois legislature in 1912 and was a major player in Chicago
politics for two decades, belonged to approximately 25 fraternal orders. In
an era when politicians could not purchase the visibility provided today
through advertising, fraternal societies enabled a glad-hander to meet and
greet to his heart's content.

There was no clear line between clubs and fraternal societies. But clubs were more likely to be exclusive and perhaps have reform or political orientations; fraternal societies were more likely to be national organizations with broad memberships. Fraternal societies were also more likely to perform business functions. Like the Order of St. Luke, most lodges took their burial and life insurance functions seriously. The first African-American insurance companies grew out of these and similar activities among church-related mutual benefit societies. Because companies controlled by whites charged blacks higher premiums—supposedly because they had higher mortality rates—black companies had a ready market for their products. So did African-American banks, since white banks seldom solicited business in the black community. Significantly, black banking and insurance companies first developed in the South, where black communities were larger and the color line was clearest.

The most dramatic example of how fraternal orders could evolve into financial institutions can be seen in the history of the Grand United Order of the True Reformers. William Washington Browne, an ex-slave and Union Army veteran, founded the organization in Richmond, Virginia, in 1881, with the intertwined goals of building a business and advancing the race. Secret ritual, regalia, a grand annual convention with a colorful

Black-owned banks served both individuals and businesses. Most white banks generally discouraged black customers, and by 1914 approximately 50 black-owned banks served African-American communities.

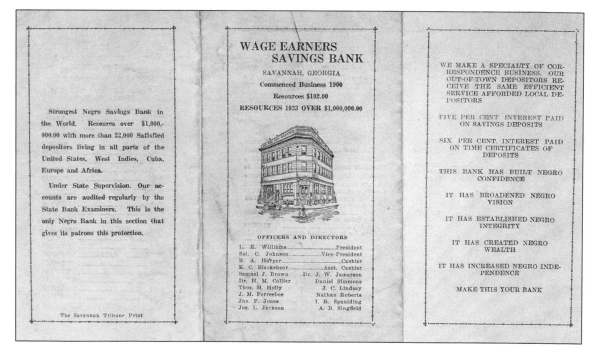

Strongest Negro Savings Bank in the World. Resources over $1,000,000.00 with more than 22,000 Satisfied depositors living in all parts of the United States, West Indies, Cuba, Europe and Africa.

Under State Supervision. Our accounts are audited regularly by the State Bank Examiners. This is the only Negro Bank in this section that gives its patrons this protection.

The Savannah Tribune Print

WAGE EARNERS SAVINGS BANK
SAVANNAH, GEORGIA
Commenced Business 1900
Resources $102.00
RESOURCES 1923 OVER $1,000,000.00

OFFICERS AND DIRECTORS
L. E. Williams _____ President
Sol. C. Johnson _____ Vice-President
R. A. Harper _____ Cashier
E. C. Blackshear _____ Asst. Cashier
Samuel J. Brown   Dr. J. W. Jamerson
Dr. H. M. Collier   Daniel Simmons
Thos. M. Holly   J. C. Lindsay
J. M. Ferreebee   Nathan Roberts
Jno. F. Jones   I. R. Spaulding
Jos. L. Jackson   A. B. Singfield

WE MAKE A SPECIALTY OF CORRESPONDENCE BUSINESS. OUR OUT-OF-TOWN DEPOSITORS RECEIVE THE SAME EFFICIENT SERVICE AFFORDED LOCAL DEPOSITORS

FIVE PER CENT. INTEREST PAID ON SAVINGS DEPOSITS

SIX PER CENT. INTEREST PAID ON TIME CERTIFICATES OF DEPOSITS

THIS BANK HAS BUILT NEGRO CONFIDENCE

IT HAS BROADENED NEGRO VISION

IT HAS ESTABLISHED NEGRO INTEGRITY

IT HAS CREATED NEGRO WEALTH

IT HAS INCREASED NEGRO INDEPENDENCE

MAKE THIS YOUR BANK

parade: each provided members with opportunities for camaraderie and ceremony within an organization also dedicated to community service. At the same time, Browne's wife found a way to earn profits with a regalia factory that she established in the True Reformers' building.

From the beginning the order's mission included mutual benefit activities. The insurance business grew so rapidly that by 1888 Browne saw an opportunity in the need to deposit and invest the cash it generated. By the turn of the century, the True Reformers counted 100,000 members and had expanded into real estate, printing, and undertaking in addition to operating an old-age home and a hotel. All catered to a black clientele.

North and South, there was a noticeable rise in black business enterprise at the beginning of the 20th century. To a considerable extent this bustling business activity was the result of the increasing segregation of African Americans into urban ghettos. But it also was part of a broader change in the social and economic life of urban black America.

In the 19th century black businessmen and even professionals had enjoyed a small white clientele in many cities. These men constituted an elite, an "upper crust," within their communities. Their social networks were generally distinct from those of other African Americans. In many cities, especially in the North, they worshipped at black churches (or in a few cases even predominantly white churches) affiliated with "white" denominations: Episcopalians, Presbyterians, Congregationalists. This group would remain the "upper crust" of black America, but by the turn of the century it was giving way to a new business and professional class, men and women who made their living serving an African-American clientele.

This transition in community leadership was personified in the career of John Merrick, a former slave who accumulated savings as a barber and owner of six barbershops in Durham, North Carolina. Merrick also sold insurance for the True Reformers. His prosperity, however, was due in large part to the stability and status provided by his position as personal barber to the white tobacco magnate James Buchanan Duke. He parlayed this stake into a much larger fortune during the first decade of the 20th century, when he drew on his experience with the True Reformers to join with two other African-American entrepreneurs to form the North Carolina Mutual Life Insurance Company.

Southern cities like Durham led the way in the growth of an African-American business class catering to African-American consumers. The largest enterprises were insurance companies and banks, but small shops were the most common form of black enterprise. What mattered to the mainly black clientele was how they were treated—with respect and in a businesslike fashion. A woman could not try on a hat in a Southern downtown store; once it sat on her head it was a "Negro hat" (or worse, a "nigger hat") that the white shop owner could not in good conscience sell to a white customer. At the pharmacy a black druggist did not expect his customers to bow and scrape, or to stand aside until all the white customers were served.

Making a virtue out of necessity, many influential black Southerners declared that the race's future lay in a "group economy." Black businesses catering to black customers would employ black men and women, creating a racial self-sufficiency rather than the individual self-sufficiency envisioned by so many rural black Southerners since emancipation.

In most cases, however, such businesses were precarious enterprises whose owners had little extra cash for emergencies or to tide them over during the occasional slow months. The limited clientele had little to spend and often needed short-term credit to weather bouts of unemployment. Retail shops sold small items, more likely to be priced in cents than in dollars. Corner groceries, barber shops, beauty parlors: all were unstable operations. Retail businesses were especially risky because whites (often European immigrants with few other business opportunities) could open

Lewis & Sons Movers in Cleveland helped black newcomers settle into their new homes.

stores in black neighborhoods and compete, largely because they had greater access to borrowed money and supplies. Barbering, undertaking, and beauty shops, on the other hand, did not face competition from white entrepreneurs reluctant to deal with black bodies.

One of the manufacturing opportunities open to black entrepreneurs lay in supplying cosmetics to African-American beauticians. Among the earliest of these manufacturers was Madam C. J. Walker, a St. Louis laundress who in the 1890s developed the first commercially successful hair-straightening process. The daughter of ex-slaves, she grew up in Mississippi as Sarah Breedlove; she later took her name from her second husband, Charles Joseph Walker. By the 1910s the Madam C. J. Walker Manufacturing Company stood at the center of an empire of approximately 20,000 managers, sales agents, clerks, and factory workers. Walker, who died in 1919, was probably the first African-American woman to join the ranks of American millionaires.

Madam C. J. Walker was probably the first African-American woman to become a millionaire.

THE GIFT OF THE GOOD FAIRY

ONCE upon a time there lived a Good Fairy whose daily thoughts were of pretty little boys and girls and of beautiful women and handsome men and of how she might make beautiful those unfortunate ones whom nature had not given long, wavy hair and a smooth, lovely complexion. So she waved her magic wand and immediately gave to those who would be beautiful a group of preparations known from that time, fifteen years ago, until to-day at home and abroad as

MADAM C. J. WALKER'S SUPERFINE PREPARATIONS FOR THE HAIR AND FOR THE SKIN

Wonderful Hair Grower	Vanishing Cream
Glossine	Cleansing Cream
Temple Grower	Cold Cream
Tetter Salve	Antiseptic Hand Soap
Vegetable Shampoo	Complexion Soap

Superfine Face Powder (white, rose-flesh, brown)
Floral Cluster Talcum Powder
Antiseptic Dental Cream
Witch Hazel Jelly

Results from the use of our preparations especially noticeable in the hair and skin of children.

Very liberal trial treatment sent anywhere upon receipt of a dollar and a half.

THE MADAM C. J. WALKER MFG. CO.
640 North West Street   *Dept. 1-X*   Indianapolis, Indiana

Walker's business success was unusual, but not unique. Other African Americans accumulated fortunes in the cosmetics business, in some cases opening schools to train beauticians in their particular method and, of course, tying that method to a particular line of products. Anthony Overton established the Overton Hygienic Manufacturing Company in Kansas City, Kansas, in 1898 and moved the company to Chicago in 1911. Sales of such products as High Brown Face Powder provided him with sufficient resources to diversify into real estate development and journalism. But all of this remained within a black world. Overton developed property in Chicago's South Side ghetto, known to many as "Bronzeville"; his newspaper, the *Chicago Bee,* had few white readers or advertisers.

This business class, however, remained small. With an even smaller professional class, and many businessmen barely holding on, the top of the class structure of urban black communities was extremely limited. Except at the very highest levels, status tended to depend less on wealth or on white definitions of occupational prestige than on notions of "refinement" and "respectability" maintained by the upper and middle classes. The few professionals tended to dominate the highest rungs, with the more secure businessmen (most were, in fact, men) close behind.

In northern cities, postal workers, porters serving railroad travelers in luxurious Pullman cars (sleeping cars with dining facilities), and servants employed by the best hotels and wealthiest white families constituted much of the solid middle class. Other workers with stable incomes and some education could also claim middle-class status. What often mattered most was property ownership, preferred leisure activities, and membership in an appropriate club, lodge, or church.

This group, based in black businesses and social institutions, seized the mantle of African-American leadership in most urban black communities around the turn of the century. They replaced the older elite whose commitment to integration sometimes led them to oppose building separate institutions to serve the community. In many cities, for example, it was clear that if blacks wanted a YMCA it would have to be a segregated institution. Banks, hospitals, professional baseball teams, social service institutions, political organizations—North and South, their existence often depended on the willingness of black communities to accept segregated institutions.

Baseball provides a typical example of the shift from slight access to white institutions to the establishment of a segregated black world. In the 19th century, a handful of black baseball players joined white athletes on professional diamonds. By the early 20th century they had been driven out, relegated to all-black barnstorming tours and marginally successful leagues.

Only after World War I, under the tenacious and imaginative leadership of Rube Foster, owner-manager of Chicago's American Giants, would the Negro National League establish a stable setting for black baseball. Black players flourished in this new arrangement, but they did so under conditions far inferior to their white counterparts'. Yet the teams constituted a source of pride to the black communities that they represented. Whatever their individual team loyalties, black fans pulled together on the few occasions when Negro League stars competed against white major leaguers.

The American Giants were formed by Andrew "Rube" Foster in 1911. Nine years later Foster founded the first stable black professional league, the Negro National League. Foster's team dominated the Negro National League during the 1920s.

These separate black institutions caused mixed feelings among black Americans. On the one hand, segregated institutions owed their existence to the exclusion of blacks from "mainstream" American life. In some cases African Americans even paid taxes for public facilities from which they were excluded. Finally, separate was almost never equal. African-American institutions such as schools, clubs, businesses, and athletic leagues nearly always lacked the facilities, money, and equipment available to their white counterparts.

At the same time, however, segregated institutions permitted community control over important cultural activities. A baseball team, a YMCA, a hospital, a retirement home—black communities could proudly claim these as their institutions maintained by and for African Americans.

79

CLASS '04 F.S.N.I.S.

CHAPTER 4

SCHOOLING FOR
LEADERSHIP

The class of 1904 of the Florida State Normal Industrial School. Black colleges varied in their orientation, with some oriented towards liberal arts and others towards vocational training in agriculture and skilled trades. Most of the colleges trained teachers, and nearly all considered it their task to train the next generation of African-American leadership.

I n the early 20th century, education was one area in which African Americans confronted the tension between the high price of segregation on the one hand and the advantages of community control on the other. Descended from slaves denied by the law any access to literacy, 20th-century African Americans recognized the importance of education in the advancement of both individuals and the race as a whole. Black children needed schooling, and black Americans needed those schools to teach the values and skills required of a new generation of men and women who would lead the march toward equality and full citizenship.

Before the Civil War most Northern states had either excluded black children from public education or shunted them into separate schools. In some cities black communities and white abolitionists established private schools for black children. During the 1870s and 1880s, however, Northern state legislatures reversed legislation requiring segregation and even went so far as to prohibit the exclusion of children from their local school on the basis of race.

By the early 20th century, many of the emerging ghettos in Northern cities were not yet sufficiently compact to enable white city officials to draw school district lines that would segregate neighborhood schools. In such cases black children attended schools that were predominantly, but not exclusively, African American. They were not the best schools their cities had to offer. They were housed in older buildings, often were overcrowded, and many of the white teachers looked down on their students. But they were decent schools, capable of providing students the opportunity to graduate from a high school that met the academic standards of the time. The schools were fully supported by tax dollars and taught by instructors with appropriate academic credentials.

Black Northerners valued these schools, and their children were less likely than the children of European immigrants to drop out as teenagers. They also valued integration, rising in protest whenever pressures emerged from segments of the white citizenry to segregate the schools. Most African Americans assumed, wisely, that the presence of whites guaranteed a certain degree of commitment from city politicians.

At the same time, however, Northern black communities had little control over what was taught or who stood in front of the classrooms. Nearly all school officials were white; so were the teachers, most of whom assumed that black children could not perform as well as their white peers. Some teachers simply assumed that the "white race" was more intelligent and more disciplined. Others who were more liberal extended sympathy to black children who they thought were crippled by the cultural heritage of African backwardness combined with the traumas of slavery. The cost of full integration into the system, even if not into completely integrated schools was clear: these were institutions *for* African Americans; but they were not African-American institutions.

By contrast, in most of the South black children went to schools staffed by black teachers and black principals. But the facilities varied from inadequate to abysmal. By the early 20th century most Southern black children had some access to a public school, but in rural areas that school was likely to be open for less than six months of the year—even as little as two months in some cases. White planters wanted black children in the fields, not wasting their time sitting on the crude benches of a one-room schoolhouse. Even into his 80s, Alabama sharecropper Ned Cobb vividly recalled having to "jump in the white man's field and work for what we could get, go choppin' cotton, go to hoein'; white folks' schools runnin right on and the white man's children goin to school while we working in his field."

In 1915, only 58 percent of all black school-age children in the South were enrolled in school at all, compared with 80 percent of whites. City kids were the most likely to be in school. Attendance rates (the proportion of enrolled children who attended each day) of black urban children lagged only slightly behind rates for whites, a remarkable comparison because few cities provided public high schools for black children.

In most Southern cities, especially in the Deep South, white civic leaders considered the education of black children an extravagance, a decision consistent with school systems that readily placed as many as 65 black children in dilapidated classrooms headed by a single teacher. The *Atlanta*

Schools in the South for African-American children suffered from inadequate facilities and high student-teacher ratios. It was not unusual for one teacher to lead a class of fifty or more children of different ages.

Constitution left little doubt as to its idea of how much schooling black children needed, defending black education on the basis of its ability to "make a better cotton picker and a more efficient plowman."

By 1915, following a decade of unprecedented expansion in high school education in the South, neither Georgia, Louisiana, Mississippi, North Carolina, nor South Carolina had yet built a high school for black teenagers. The enlightened officials of Delaware, Florida, and Maryland had established a single black high school in each of these segregated states. During this period most American communities were transforming high school from a privilege available to those who could afford private school to a right funded by the taxpayers. Southern black youth were denied that right.

Tragically, black adults were among the taxpayers who supported the very school systems that allocated them only crumbs from an expanding pie. To provide better opportunities for their children, black Southerners had to mobilize their communities and do the work themselves. In effect, they paid twice—once for a public school system that allocated them a fraction of the money available to white schools and a second time to supplement those meager resources or pay tuition at a private black high school.

In many cases the additional burden was paid with labor rather than dollars, as many black Southerners had little more than their hands, tools, and skills to spare. Thousands of black public schools in the rural South were erected in the early 20th century through donations from Chicago philanthropist Julius Rosenwald (the president of Sears, Roebuck & Company), who required that each community match his contribution dollar for dollar. In most cases public funds from white-controlled sources— that is, from taxes—amounted to less than the hard-earned cash generated within the black community. Black Southerners were known to donate their last pennies to provide opportunities for the next generation. Even people with no children would sacrifice, suggesting that the values that had nourished school-building during Reconstruction remained a central aspect of African-American culture in the South.

In addition to contributing to the construction of public schools, black Southerners built private schools, especially at the high school level. At the turn of the century three-fourths of all Southern black high school students attended a private school. Coming from grossly inadequate grammar schools, many of these students required remedial classes, further straining the already precarious budgets of these institutions.

Church-sponsored schools such as Scotia Seminary in North Carolina, founded by the Presbyterian Church in 1870, trained young women in such fields as teaching, nursing, home economics, and missionary work.

Neither public nor private schools in the South were controlled by African Americans. Public school teachers and principals had to answer to white officials, most of whom cared less about whether black children were being educated than whether they were learning anything that threatened social stability. In Palmetto, Georgia, a teacher was dismissed for merely expressing his approval when President Theodore Roosevelt invited the exceedingly moderate black leader Booker T. Washington to dinner at the White House. Elsewhere in the same state a county school board president required all black students to learn and recite "Goin' Back to Dixie." He had composed this song himself; its lyrics celebrated segregation, the South, and white supremacy.

African-American private schools owed a different kind of allegiance. Although by the early 20th century nearly all of these were headed by African Americans, they still depended on the contributions of Northern white philanthropists for a considerable portion of their budget. And in rural areas they remained vulnerable to white public opinion, which tolerated a black private school only if it clearly was not educating its students out of their place.

Northern donors generally were interested in teaching black Southerners to be good workers. Wallace Buttrick, Executive Director of the General Education Board, which funnelled millions of dollars into the South, typically pointed that funding toward "training the negro for productive efficiency." Northern philanthropists, in part because they envisioned an increasingly industrialized South with a black work force, aimed for a considerably higher level of literacy than most white Southerners thought black children would ever need.

In spite of these limits on the independence of Southern black educators, many black schools were, in fact, community institutions. Black children were taught by black teachers partly because black parents had demanded this change during the closing decades of the 19th century. White officials had given in to this demand for financial reasons: black teachers earned less than their white counterparts. But the large-scale entrance of African Americans into the teaching profession is significant nevertheless. These men and women played active roles in their communities, organizing women's clubs, farmers' clubs, boys' clubs, school improvement leagues, and various other self-improvement efforts.

African Americans looked upon schooling as a privilege—one that carried with it an obligation to use one's learning on behalf of the entire community. And teachers joined lawyers, social workers, librarians, nurses, doctors, and newspaper reporters and publishers as leaders of their community.

These educational institutions stood at the center of major divisions among black leaders about the role of African Americans in American society. All the schools taught the same basic values of industry, thrift, and service to the community. They recruited similar types of students. But curriculum and school leadership reflected different notions of how black Americans could attain full citizenship in a nation seemingly committed to their subordination. To what kinds of jobs should they aspire? How should they respond to the rising tide of segregation? Where should they look for allies? How hard should they push for immediate equality when few whites even considered African Americans capable of eventual equality?

A clear response to these questions lay in the missions of the Hampton and Tuskegee Institutes, and their many offshoots across the rural South. Unlike such liberal arts institutions as Fisk University and Atlanta University, these vocationally oriented schools disdained preparing black students to compete with whites or challenging the ideas underlying white supremacy. Instead these schools accommodated to the system, preparing students for roles within it.

Their graduates would be better farmers, successful small businessmen, or even more skilled domestic servants. They trained teachers who would fan out across the South committed to raising moral and material standards in black communities without directly confronting existing political, economic, or social arrangements.

The personification of this "accommodationist" philosophy was Booker T. Washington, the most powerful African American of the early 20th century. Washington offered his own life story, published as *Up from Slavery* in 1901, as an inspiration to his people. Born a slave in West Virginia in 1856, he labored in salt works, in coal mines, and as a servant for a locally prominent white family. He left home at the age of 16 to enroll at Hampton Institute in Virginia. Able to afford only a portion of the train fare, he hitched wagon rides and walked part of the way. In Richmond he spent a night trying to sleep under an elevated sidewalk. Washington not only reached his destination; he became Hampton's most famous graduate, going on to establish his own school in the image of his alma mater.

Tuskegee Institute, founded in 1881, became Washington's power base until his death in 1915. He cultivated the support of Northern philan-

This rolling school was given to the government agricultural extension service by African-American farmers of Alabama. It was named for Booker T. Washington, who helped set up the extension service.

thropists by promising to teach his people to be industrious workers. He promised to train a black leadership that would exhort the masses to lift themselves up by their bootstraps. He reassured local whites that his institution posed no threat to their way of life. Neither he nor anyone associated with his school would question white supremacy or the exclusion of black Southerners from politics.

Advising his people to "cast down your bucket where you are," Washington urged them to remain in place both geographically and socially. He first used this phrase in a speech to a white audience in Atlanta in 1895, at the same time affirming his acceptance of Jim Crow: "In all things that are purely social we can be as separate as the fingers, yet one as the hand in all things essential to mutual progress."

Washington's address (later dubbed the "Atlanta Compromise") catapulted him into the role of spokesman for black America, as whites found him at once reassuring to them and inspiring to his people. He celebrated the small annual increases in black land ownership and offered these gains as proof that the future of African Americans lay in Southern agriculture.

He promoted the values of his supporters in the business community, assuring blacks that political rights and social equality were less important than a demonstration of their importance to the Southern economy.

Washington was not, however, merely a puppet of his white patrons. Republican leaders in Washington and Northern philanthropists interested in the plight of African Americans turned to him for advice on how to direct their dollars to "appropriate" black institutions, or on which black politicians should receive the few appointments available to their race. Even powerful white Southerners would consult him (though never openly) for advice on which Negroes might be considered "safe" for appointments as public school principals or teachers.

By the turn of the century the "Tuskegee Machine" exercised considerable influence—if often indirectly—over institutions across black America. Scores of Southern private schools operated on the Tuskegee model, with principals and teachers occupying influential positions in small communities. In cities across the nation, African-American newspapers, many with direct subsidies from Tuskegee, trumpeted Washington's successes. His National Negro Business League, founded in 1900 to encourage black enterprise (and black patronage of black businesses), grew to 320 branches within eight years. Like Washington's other public initiatives, the league confined its political activity to the politics of advancement through

Booker T. Washington addresses an Abraham Lincoln memorial ceremony at New York's Carnegie Hall in 1906. Author Mark Twain is third from left, front row on the stage. Washington also used Carnegie Hall for a fundraiser for Tuskegee Institute.

individual and racial self-help. Its conventions "attended strictly to business"; electoral politics and public protest had no place on the agenda.

Ironically, politics was in fact always on Washington's agenda. But it was a politics of leadership within the African-American community rather than a politics that challenged racism, discrimination, or the exclusion of blacks from voting booths. Although Washington apparently worked behind the scenes in the fight against disfranchisement and segregation, he fought mostly to win and retain his place at the top of a separate African-American institutional world.

Washington's popularity and influence among black Americans owed much to the eagerness of powerful whites to promote him as a spokesman and emissary. His stature derived from his visibility, from the impulse among black Americans to be proud of someone who had seemingly overcome the obstacles of racism to build institutions and sit at the table with the rich and powerful.

When President Theodore Roosevelt invited Booker T. Washington to dine with him at the White House in 1901, millions of black Americans claimed a victory. It mattered only to a very few that Washington had been chosen both because of his moderation and because Roosevelt considered him an exceptional Negro, different from others of his "inferior" race.

Washington's gospel of hard work, landownership, self-help, and success through small business struck genuine chords among most black Americans. To some, however, the Atlanta Compromise conceded too much. John Hope, a young Southern educator and future college president, considered it "cowardly and dishonest for any of our colored men to tell white people or colored people that we are not struggling for equality."

William Monroe Trotter, editor of the *Boston Guardian* (founded in 1901), was even more scathing. Washington's willingness to accommodate to Jim Crow, along with his success in forging alliances with white businessmen, proclaimed Trotter, exposed him as "a coward" and a "self seeker." He was "the Benedict Arnold of the Negro race, the Exploiter of Exploiters, the Great Traitor," Trotter wrote. Trotter heckled Washington mercilessly at a speech in Boston in 1903, relenting only after the police had removed him from the hall.

That same year a more measured—and eventually more influential—challenge to Washington emerged in the form of a book, *The Souls of Black Folk*. The author, W. E. B. Du Bois, shared the widespread "Washingtonian" faith in self-help, racial solidarity, respectability, and thrift. He had little quarrel with the Tuskegee approach to educating the masses, for whom industrial education and teacher training was essential and useful.

But Du Bois believed African Americans needed more and were entitled to the same educational opportunities as their white peers. The development of black leadership required the availability of a first-class liberal arts education comparable to what was available at elite white colleges. Indeed, such an education would provide the elites of both races with the humane values necessary to overcome racism. Washington envisioned the dollar as the eventual currency of a democracy that valued everyone for what they could earn rather than according to the color of their skin. Du Bois envisioned a common currency of values: justice, truth, and the aesthetic and moral bases of civic culture.

Du Bois taught sociology at Atlanta University and wrote movingly in *The Souls of Black Folk* of the cultural heritage of the black rural South. But his faith that any sort of progress was possible in the South was dwindling. He complained about "narrow repression" and "provincialism." Washington had it backward, Du Bois declared. It was not the dollar that provided dignity, but citizenship. And citizenship required the political and legal rights denied to black Southerners.

W. E. B. Du Bois was a much-sought speaker on the African-American lecture circuit. His comment soon after the turn of the century that "the problem of the twentieth century is the problem of the color line," was both an insight into current conditions and a prediction of things to come.

Du Bois, Trotter, and Hope stood out as spokesmen for a more militant response to the rising tide of racism, but they hardly stood alone. Residents of Southern cities, many of them people who admired Washington and acknowledged his distinction, participated in boycotts of Jim Crow streetcars between 1898 and 1904. In a few instances black Southerners even filed unsuccessful court suits challenging the legality of segregation ordinances.

In the North, where 19th-century black elites had developed ties to prominent whites and participated in a handful of integrated institutions (including high schools, colleges, political organizations, and an occasional club or philanthropic society), an older generation refused to abandon the goal of integration. The younger men and women of this class were less influential within the community than the

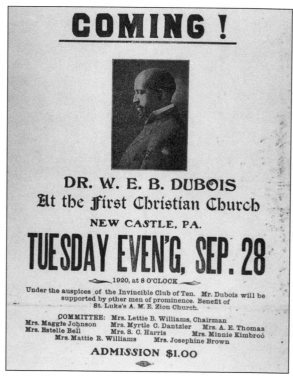

90

rising class of black business and professional people catering to a black clientele. Nonetheless, many of this younger black middle class remained loyal to their parents' ideals and emerged as some of Washington's most articulate critics.

Moreover, despite Washington's ability to influence the editorial policies of most black newspapers, Trotter's was not the only militant editorial voice. Harry T. Smith, editor of the *Cleveland Gazette,* not only assailed any evidence of racial discrimination but he denounced the establishment of black facilities meant to provide services that comparable white institutions refused to provide to African Americans. He and others of like mind in Northern cities insisted that to build a black facility made it easier for the whites to maintain their policies of exclusion. Chicago's black leadership had rejected a segregated YMCA in 1889 on these principles. Smith dismissed Washington's Atlanta Compromise as a "doctrine of surrender."

Mary Church Terrell devoted much of her adult life to the struggle for civil rights for African Americans and women. The first president of the National Association of Colored Women, she also was active in public school reform and the Republican party.

For much of the African-American leadership at the beginning of the century, politics involved more than a choice between racial integration or self-help, protest or accommodation, liberal or vocational education. Alliances shifted. Lines were never neat and clean. Du Bois broke with Washington eight years after the Atlanta Compromise speech. Mary Church Terrell publicly supported Washington while fighting for suffrage—for African Americans and for women.

A graduate of Oberlin College, Terrell supported both Tuskegee and Du Bois's Atlanta University. As president of the National Association of Colored Women she also maintained a working relationship with Margaret Murray Washington (Booker T. Washington's wife) and other women in the generally moderate women's club movement. Ida B. Wells, a suffragist, antilynching activist, and militant advocate of civil rights, broke with Washington in 1899 and remained a bitter critic of his efforts to accommodate to Jim Crow and attempts to control black institutions and newspapers.

Robert Abbott, editor of the *Chicago Defender,* was a graduate of Hampton Institute who believed that all black children should learn a trade and advised black Southerners to "stick to the farm." He admired Washington and praised Tuskegee as a great black institution. At the same time his headlines offered very un-Washingtonian advice to black Southerners:

"WHEN THE MOB COMES AND YOU MUST DIE TAKE AT LEAST ONE WITH YOU."

Yet there were occasions when black people felt they had to line up, to take a particular position. Led by Du Bois and Trotter, a small group, nearly all from the North and mostly urban college graduates, met in 1905 to form the Niagara Movement. The movement was named for its meeting place on the Canadian side of Niagara Falls, a major terminus of the Underground Railroad. Du Bois had encountered difficulty arranging hotel accommodations on the American side. The following year the group met at Harpers Ferry, West Virginia, the site of John Brown's famous raid on behalf of abolitionism.

The Niagara Movement denounced white racism and demanded full citizenship for blacks and the abolition of all racial distinctions. At the same time it underscored the increasingly significant double bind facing African-American workers: industrial employers hired them only as temporary strikebreakers, and most unions excluded them from membership.

Two events in 1906 underscored the immediacy of the Niagara Movement's agenda, while at the same time pointing to the ineffectiveness of black protest up to this point. In August of that year President Roosevelt ordered the dishonorable discharge of three companies of black soldiers after they were accused of inciting a riot in Brownsville, Texas. Evidence of their responsibility was thin at best. They were more likely victims of violence than instigators. Their mistake, apparently, was in fighting back.

Roosevelt's "executive lynching" demonstrated that black Americans had few friends in high places. They had even fewer in the streets. In Atlanta, a month after the Brownsville incident and following a spate of local newspaper articles that fictitiously reported assaults on white women by black men, a mob of more than 10,000 white citizens freely attacked African Americans. The attacks continued for five days, and the police generally refused to interfere. The city's white establishment blamed the riot on irresponsible journalism and overreaction by lower-class whites. But most white Atlantans shared the mayor's conclusion that the bottom line was "black brutes [who] attempt rape upon our women." Once again, whites associated lynching with rape when in fact there had been no rape.

By 1908, the Niagara Movement's weakness was as obvious as its astute analysis of the crisis of American race relations. Few of the movement's 400 members bothered to pay dues; most of the black press ignored

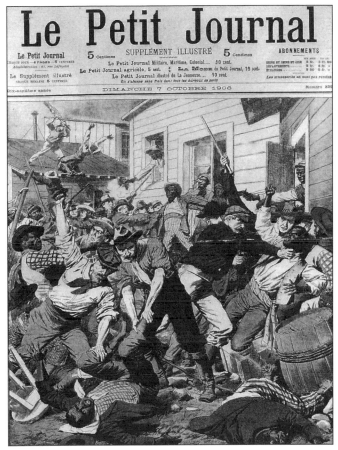

it as a handful of cranky elitists hurling manifestos. Whites paid even less attention.

The Niagara Movement represents a turning point because of its view of race relations in the United States and its militant agenda for change. Its collapse coincided with an event that shocked the small portion of the Northern white population that considered racism a major "problem" in American life: lynchings and mob attacks on African Americans in Springfield, Illinois. The violence was ignited by a spark recognizable to anyone familiar with the behavior of Southern lynch mobs: a white woman had accused a black workman of rape (she later recanted, admitting that a white man whom she refused to name had beaten her). When the authorities removed the accused man from town to protect him from enraged white citizens, a mob gathered, determined to

The French newspaper Le Petit Journal *reported extensively on lynchings and other examples of racial conflict in the United States.*

make the black community pay a price for its supposed tolerance of such criminal behavior. Five thousand soldiers were required to restore order after whites attacked black businesses, homes, and individuals.

White Northerners had condemned the Atlanta riot but had explained away the terrorism by blaming it on the peculiar backwardness of the South. But in Abraham Lincoln's hometown, on the centennial of the Great Emancipator's birth? This event pushed the minority of white reformers who already had begun to question Booker T. Washington's accommodationist agenda to consider the views of Du Bois and the "radicals."

In 1910, the remnants of the Niagara Movement joined with a small group of reformers—mostly white—who had met the previous year in response to the Springfield riot. Their new organization, the National Association for the Advancement of Colored People (NAACP), began with a straightforward agenda: to secure the basic citizenship rights guaranteed by the 14th and 15th Amendments to the United States Constitution. Most specifically this meant the end of all segregation laws, a right to equal education, and a guarantee of the right to vote.

The NAACP would publicize discrimination whenever and wherever it occurred, lobby legislatures and Congress for civil rights legislation, and file lawsuits grounded in constitutional law. It also launched a campaign against lynching, which used research and on-site reports to undermine the standard Southern defense of lynching—that its real cause was black criminality and uncontrolled sexuality. Tame by 20th-century standards, the NAACP departed significantly from Washington's accommodationism.

Like the Niagara Movement, the NAACP was led mainly by elites. But it also sparked enthusiasm among two groups that the Niagara radicals had not tapped: the black middle and working classes, and white liberals. Although Du Bois was the only African American in the original "inner circle" of the organization, African Americans dominated the membership from the beginning. By 1918 the NAACP monthly magazine, the *Crisis* (founded and edited by Du Bois), claimed a circulation of 100,000. In the rural South many enthusiasts read and circulated the journal at considerable risk.

The first issue of The Crisis, *the official magazine of the NAACP that was edited by W. E. B. Du Bois. By 1918 the magazine's circulation had reached 100,000 copies per month.*

J. W. Townsend, a black schoolteacher outside Rison, Arkansas, who was arrested for selling the Christmas issue, was typical of a growing number of local opinion leaders across the South. Active NAACP membership might be suicidal, but support for the organization was crucial. As African Americans like James Weldon Johnson and Walter White moved into more leadership roles after 1916 and local branches multiplied, the organization solidified its place at the center of the African-American protest movement for the next half-century.

Equally crucial—and more controversial—was the level of white involvement, especially in the early years. Disdainful of efforts that depended on white goodwill, William Monroe Trotter remained skeptical of the organization's potential and kept his distance. Men and women at the other end of the

THE CRISIS
A RECORD OF THE DARKER RACES

Volume One   NOVEMBER, 1910   Number One

Edited by W. E. BURGHARDT DU BOIS, with the co-operation of Oswald Garrison Villard, J. Max Barber, Charles Edward Russell, Kelly Miller, W. S. Braithwaite and M. D. Maclean.

CONTENTS

Along the Color Line	3
Opinion	7
Editorial	10
The N. A. A. C. P.	12
Athens and Brownsville	13
By MOORFIELD STOREY	
The Burden	14
What to Read	15

PUBLISHED MONTHLY BY THE
National Association for the Advancement of Colored People
AT TWENTY VESEY STREET   NEW YORK CITY

ONE DOLLAR A YEAR   TEN CENTS A COPY

This cartoon, entitled "The Next Colored Delegation to the White House," appeared in The Crisis *in 1916. It ridiculed the racist views of President Woodrow Wilson, a native of Virginia.*

social spectrum from the Harvard-educated Trotter were probably equally skeptical.

But the great portion of black leadership was moving toward a position best articulated by Ida B. Wells. Wells identified power as the bottom line. Washington was right in arguing that it was useless to wait for whites to help. Blacks should build whatever economic power they could. And he was right, she said, to argue that it was foolish to forget that power lay in white hands and that any strategy had to recognize that blacks were playing a weak hand. But Wells took this analysis a step further. She insisted that militant protest was both possible and effective if it could reach an audience of potentially sympathetic whites. America did not have a "Negro problem," she explained. It had a white problem.

Lessons · of · the · Hour

BY

Hon. Frederick Douglass,

Metropolitan A. M. E. Church,

WASHINGTON, D. C.

BALTIMORE:
Press of Thomas & Evans.
1894.

CHAPTER 5

THE "SECOND EMANCIPATION"

O n August 25, 1893, Frederick Douglass stood wearily
before a large audience at the World's Columbian
Exposition in Chicago. The former abolitionist, journalist,
and Republican politician had been chosen to deliver the
principal address on the occasion of "Colored American
Day" at the fair. The "Day" itself was controversial among African
Americans. Many viewed the gesture as token recognition insufficient to
compensate for their exclusion from planning and presenting exhibits.
Separate, unequal, and subordinate, the special day smacked of Jim Crow.

Ida B. Wells advised African Americans to stay away from the exposition completely. Douglass shared Wells's anger; he had contributed to her
eloquent pamphlet, *The Reason Why the Colored American Is Not in the
World's Columbian Exposition*. But the aging orator was reluctant to pass
up the chance to expose American hypocrisy on an international stage. He
denounced the nation that, proud of its own freedom, denied meaningful
freedom to many of its own citizens. "There is no Negro Problem,"
Douglass proclaimed, only the problem of Americans refusing to "live up to
their own Constitution."

Douglass's long career was coming to a close in 1893. With the
approach of a new century he was passing the mantle of leadership to a
new generation. Wells, Booker T. Washington, and W. E. B. Du Bois had
already claimed roles in this African-American vanguard. They would eventually be joined by a member of Douglass's audience, a young Georgian
who would emerge as the voice of hope for tens of thousands of black
Southerners, a "Black Moses," in the words of his biographer. His name
was Robert Sengstacke Abbott.

*"Lessons of the
Hour" was a fervent
protest against the
epidemic of lynchings
of black citizens. "In
its thirst for blood
and its rage for
vengeance," Douglass
said, "the mob has
blindly, boldly and
defiantly supplanted
sheriffs, constables
and police."*

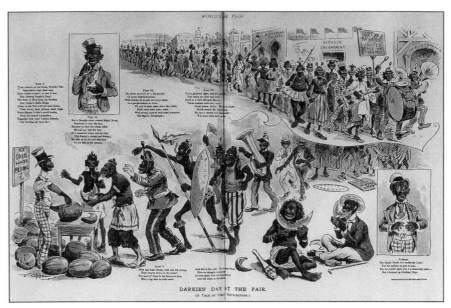

DARKIES' DAY AT THE FAIR.
(A TALE OF PURE RETRIBUTION.)

This cartoon, "Darkies' Day at the Fair," appeared in the British humor magazine Puck. *It satirized the display of Africans at the World's Columbian Exposition in Chicago in 1893, which Frederick Douglass and other African Americans found extremely offensive.*

Abbott came to the fair not to agitate but to entertain. Taking his place on the stage with the other three members of a vocal quartet from Hampton Institute, the 25-year-old tenor was as captivated by the Windy City itself as he was by the inspiring words of Douglass and the excitement of performing at the great exposition. Like thousands of other fair visitors Abbott sensed that the future lay in Chicago.

After learning the printer's trade at Hampton, Abbott returned to Chicago in 1897, hoping to begin a career as a journalist. Ida B. Wells had resettled in Chicago two years earlier, resuming her career as a crusader against lynching and a journalist. That two ambitious young African Americans would share this interest is not surprising. In the tradition of Douglass, who had been the editor and publisher of a major abolitionist newspaper, the African-American press stood at the center of black American urban life and politics in the early 20th century. Even in the rural South, religious newspapers permitted communication across county and state lines, connecting African-American communities to one another.

Links between communities were strongest within the South, where African Americans moved from place to place, visited and corresponded with relatives, and sought news from itinerant preachers and migrant laborers. Men traveled from job to job; even a preacher moved from pulpit to pulpit. Less dependent on itinerant employment, women more frequently traveled to visit.

In the South, black newspapers filled columns with brief, but revealing, articles, usually noting when a woman—or occasionally a single man—was visiting relatives. A reader of the *Norfolk Journal and Guide,* for example, would learn that "Mr. Lonnie Jones, Norfolk, visited his parents, the Rev. and Mrs. Jones in Durham, North Carolina." These items were more than "filler"; readers wanted to know where people came from and who they visited. The linkage of family life, generation to generation, across distances great and small had become an important part of African-American culture.

The idea of movement itself, an important theme in American history in general, has held special significance to the African-American experience. Upon emancipation many former slaves had tested their freedom by moving, if only a few miles to the next plantation. The impulse and its significance were so powerful that 65 years later, a woman declared an end to an interview about her early years as a slave by asserting her freedom to come and go. "I can go when I please and come back when I please. I'll come to see you, I must go home now. I am a free rooster." From emancipation well into the 20th century, African-American musical lyrics were laced with comments about "goin' down dat lonesome road," or "I got up this morning and I wash my face, / Goin' to eat breakfast in a bran' new place." As the legendary bluesman Robert Johnson put it,

> I got to keep moving, I got to keep moving,
> Blues falling down like hail, blues falling down like hail.

Merely thinking about moving could boost the endurance of black workers who recognized that limited opportunities meant that moving along—rather than moving up—would eventually provide relief from their toil—at least until they began work someplace else. Work itself was fused with the idea of movement through work songs that set the pace of labor, in this case among a sawmill crew:

> OH–OH–In the morning;
> OH OH In the evening;
> OH–OH–Hallelujah!
> Ain't gonna be here all my days.

If not here, then where? For men, sawmills, turpentine camps, phosphate mines, and coal mines provided endless opportunities to move from place to place. Some were merely looking for work during breaks in the agricultural routine. Others sought liberation from farm life entirely. Cities promised more community life but fewer jobs, except in places like Birmingham, Alabama, where the steel mills provided unusual (though still limited) industrial opportunities. Women, always in demand as servants and laundresses, could more easily find stable employment. Families could, and did, move to the coal towns stretching across Appalachia south toward Birmingham. However, the instability of employment in timber, turpentine, and most other industries open to African Americans was unattractive to workers trying to raise children. Some sought agricultural opportunities farther south in Florida, or—more often—west to the Mississippi Delta, Arkansas, and Texas. These destinations within the South drew African Americans who either persisted in their hopes to attain independence through land ownership or whose frustration kept them on the move but with no other apparent alternative.

Frustration and alienation, however, could also provide the foundation for hope, for faith in the ability of black people to turn their backs on their "white problem" and build their own alternatives. Some were attracted to a growing movement to establish "black towns," mainly in Oklahoma, but also as far west as Allensworth, California. Promoters of these communities, generally men who stood to profit from the sale of land, often combined business motivations with a strong belief in racial self-help.

African Americans founded approximately 25 black towns in Oklahoma between 1891 and 1910, promising residents an opportunity to live free from white influence or interference. Business, government, and all other institutions were controlled from within each town. But an existence

The town council of Boley, Oklahoma. Black towns offered African Americans opportunities for self-government in the early 20th century.

apart from whites was impossible. A market economy demanded money, and few blacks could bring substantial resources to these enterprises. Moreover, in 1907 Oklahoma became a state, one that looked distinctly Southern in its rush to disfranchise black voters. Even as black Southerners continued to make their way into Oklahoma, despair and disillusion was leading some of the earlier pioneers to look beyond American borders.

The most common, and most enduring destination for potential black emigrants was Liberia. This West African nation was originally colonized before the Civil War by African Americans under the auspices of antislavery—and anti-Negro—whites who considered exportation of blacks the solution to the evils of slavery. Liberia took on a different image later in the century, as a haven from American racism.

By 1910 thousands of black Americans had bought shares in joint stock companies promising passage across the Atlantic. Others joined emigration clubs, listened with interest to speeches about Liberia, or read newspapers advocating emigration. But much of this enthusiasm, which seemed to rise during especially low points in Southern race relations, took hold among men and women too poor to actually book passage or keep the back-to-Africa movement alive.

For most black Southerners, therefore, leaving the South meant moving north. And moving to the North meant the city. Northern farmland was expensive and most Northern rural communities expressed sympathy for oppressed blacks only as long as they remained oppressed *Southern* blacks.

Even in cities, as Robert Abbott learned, opportunities varied from nonexistent to scarce. Like other African-American craftsmen, most of

Teachers and students of Liberia College.

whom had been trained in the South, this skilled printer found it impossible to find regular employment in a Northern city. Abbott took short-term printing jobs while attending Kent College of Law at night—the only African American in his graduating class. But the Chicago bar was no more hospitable to blacks than most of the city's neighborhood bars.

The rapidly growing metropolis of nearly 2 million people needed plenty of attorneys, but African-American legal business for the most part had to be generated by the small black community of 30,000 people. An established core of black attorneys left little space for outsiders. Even within that community, Abbott found that his skin color put him at a disadvantage. A prominent African-American lawyer once curtly informed him that he was too dark to be effective in a courtroom.

Abbott returned to irregular employment as a printer, but with a larger goal in mind. On a May evening in 1905, he appeared on the streets of black Chicago selling the four-page *Chicago Defender,* which on its front page proclaimed itself "The World's Greatest Weekly." He began with virtually no money; the publisher and editor was also the reporting staff, business manager, and sales force. His landlady's kitchen table doubled as his desk.

Although the obstacles facing Robert Abbott illustrate the difficulties confronting black newcomers to Northern cities in the early years of the century, his actual experience was unusual. Black Southerners struggled mightily to provide their children with a decent education, but few young men or women reached the heights of a secondary or college degree. Moreover, Hampton, Tuskegee, and their offshoots encouraged graduates to remain in the South, to assume positions of leadership in their communities.

Black Southerners did move North during the early years of the 20th century, but they did so in small numbers. Most came from the border states rather than such Deep South states as Abbott's native Georgia. Educated or uneducated, urban or rural, male or female, black Southerners who thought about the possibility of a better life elsewhere had to face the reality that earning a decent living in the North was close to impossible.

After building the *Defender* into a stable business, Abbott turned to the region of his birth and advised black Southerners that they should confront Southern racism rather than try to escape it. "The only wise thing to do," he declared in 1915, "is to stick to the farm." By then, however, increasing numbers of black Southerners were finding this advice difficult—if not impossible—to follow. A series of natural disasters during the preceding decade had struck with particular force in the cotton belt. In addition to boll weevils who "eat up all de cotton," drought followed by flood plagued Southern farmers. Consecutive years of poor crops in some counties had made it difficult for farmers to obtain credit, a necessity for tenants and owners of small farms. Hard times, however, were nothing new for black Southerners. They had endured Jim Crow for a generation. Most knew no life other than one of hard work with poverty as its reward. It is unlikely that a substantial number would have left the South as a result of these setbacks.

Something new was happening, however, in the North. The beginning of World War I in Europe in 1914 sent shock waves across the Atlantic, stimulating the American economy while shutting off its traditional source of industrial labor. American manufacturers could earn astronomical profits, selling first to the European combatants and, by 1916, to a domestic market on the verge of conversion to a wartime economy. But where would the additional workers be recruited? The war had stopped immigration from Europe. Within a year American entry into the war would divert thousands of men from the labor force to the armed forces. New sources of labor would have to be found.

Labor shortages hit first on the railroads, which were traditional employers of large numbers of casual laborers. By 1916 these men could find more secure and lucrative jobs in factories. Before railroad companies would turn to African Americans, however, they had to exhaust other alternatives. Some railroad executives assumed that they could recruit Mexicans to perform the regular track maintenance required every spring in the Northeast and Midwest. Other railroad executives looked to a different labor source. "By starting track work early," one executive explained, it would be possible to complete this chore with "American labor. The American hobo caught in the spring of the year will work."

Leaving aside this common assumption that the category "American" did not include African-American workers, such approaches reveal that employers considered the shortage temporary, requiring little rethinking of traditional assumptions about the ability of black men to do a "white man's job." Referring to employment patterns in Northern cities, the magazine *New Republic* observed in mid-1916 that "the Negro gets a chance to work only when there is no one else."

The notion of "no one else" depended not only on ideas about race, but also about gender. Many employers first reconsidered whether white

A chain gang clad in prison stripes does maintenance on a streetcar line in Atlanta. Chain gangs combined public humiliation with hard physical labor and were frequently used in the South during the first half of the twentieth century.

man's work was necessarily man's work. During World War I thousands of white women moved into meat packinghouses, munitions and chemical factories, electrical industries, and other workplaces previously reserved for their husbands, fathers, and brothers. But stereotypes about gender were powerful, and employers generally considered women unsuitable for most types of industrial work.

In the packinghouses, for example, women could stuff and pack sausages but they were considered incapable of such tasks as herding animals, butchering, or lugging meat. To keep the production lines running, therefore, industrialists were forced to experiment with employing black men, generally referred to as "the Negro." The experiment spread to black women when new opportunities for white women left jobs open at the bottom of the hierarchy of female work. For the first time in American history, the nation's basic industries offered production jobs to African Americans. From New York, Boston, and Philadelphia to Pittsburgh, Chicago, Detroit, and to a lesser extent Los Angeles, factory gates opened.

Work in railroad yards, steel mills, food processing plants, garment shops, and other industries paid wages far beyond what was available in the rural or urban South. But it was more than the money that attracted black Southerners north. These jobs also represented portals into the industrial economy. These opportunities promised a new basis for claims to full citizenship—a promise that a previous generation of black Southerners had envisioned in the possibility of landownership. "There is no advancement here for me," declared a black Texan in 1917. "I would like to come where

I can better my condition I woant work and not affraid to work all I wish is a chance to make good."

So they moved, approximately 500,000 black Southerners between 1916 and 1919, with twice that many following during the 1920s. This movement, known as the "Great Migration," would ebb and flow until the 1970s, shifting the center of gravity of African-American culture from the rural South to the urban North. Southern cities drew increasing numbers of men and women from surrounding counties, many of whom stayed only long enough to earn enough money to move north. Employment in the coal mines of Appalachia drew thousands of others. Smaller numbers headed west, especially toward Los Angeles, which by 1900 had surpassed San Francisco as the largest African-American community in that region. But the best opportunities and the highest wages lay in the North. Migration to a Southern city offered nothing to people like the man from Anne Mantl, Alabama, who was "disgusted with the South" and hoped to bring north a group of men who "just want a chance." What the North offered was a new start; Robert Abbott called the Great Migration a "second emancipation."

The men and women who translated the opening of new opportunities into a vast population movement had good reason for their optimism. These were not refugees blown across the winds of historical change. Rather, this was a movement of men and women who first sought information and then traveled established routes to destinations already inhabited by friends or relatives.

The depot of the Illinois Central Railroad in Chicago, where many Southern blacks got their first taste of the North.

"I like my fellow southerner am looking northward," wrote a "man of sober habits" (as he called himself) from Pensacola, Florida. But before he would leave he wanted "to know just wher I am goin and what Im to do if posible." An even more cautious migrant from Keatchie, Loui-siana, first inquired not only "about general conditions, as to wages, cost of living, living conditions etc.," but "also as to persons of color adapting themselves to the northern climate."

These letters, typical of the thousands written by black Southerners before their departure for the North, reveal the magnitude of a decision to leave home and family. They also suggest the networks of people and institutions that made the process easier. In the earliest months of the Great Migration—the fall and winter of 1916–17—recruiters working for Northern industry attracted attention in the South with stories of high wages and better living conditions in the North. Many of these recruiters were actually black workers visiting "home" with instructions (and cash incentives) from employers to recruit "reliable" friends and relatives.

In other cases black Southerners readily accepted offers of jobs and even free transportation only because they had already heard from other African Americans about the new opportunities and the differences in race relations. Men working in railroad yards and on trains, for example, could readily spread information along the tracks. Blues musician Tampa Red remembered Pullman car porters traveling through Florida describing Chicago as "God's country."

Chicago enjoyed a special reputation, because it was the home of the best-selling black newspaper in the South, the *Chicago Defender*. Fearless, sensational, and militant, Robert Abbott's newspaper expressed a perspective that was dangerous, if not impossible, for black Southerners to maintain in the presence of whites. Red ink announced lynchings, and readers were encouraged to fight back:

WHEN THE MOB COMES
AND YOU MUST DIE TAKE
AT LEAST ONE WITH YOU.

Abbott's advice shifted focus when jobs became available in Northern cities. Like other business leaders in Northern black communities he recognized that migration from the South promised opportunity not only for migrants, but also for African-American businesses and political interests. He became the primary cheerleader for "The Exodus," at one point fueling the bandwagon by setting a specific date for people to participate in a

"Great Northern Drive." Read aloud in churches, barbershops, poolrooms, and other gathering places, the *Defender, New York Age, Pittsburgh Courier,* and other black newspapers shaped black Southerners' images of what they would find in the North.

Along with the authority of newspapers, black Southerners could look to friends and relatives as trusted sources of information. Like immigrants from other nations, Southerners established migration "chains," linking those who left to those who stayed behind. The first people to leave a town often functioned as scouts for the whole community. Letters quickly followed, and often visits as well. Seeking to relate "true facts," many letters spoke of noise, dirt, high costs of living, and homesickness amidst their enthusiasm for the chance to earn money and "ride in the electric street and steam cars any where I get a seat." A recent arrival in Akron, Ohio, put it succinctly: "I work like a man. I am making good."

Innumerable other links joined North and South, city and country. Fraternal organizations and church conventions met in different cities each year, providing opportunities to visit, see the sights, and listen to hosts brag. Returning home for weddings, funerals, or just to show off their accomplishments, migrants flaunted city clothes and spoke of voting, going to big-league baseball games, and passing white people on the street without having to step into the gutter.

Energized by such powerful images, ambitious Southerners moved north with a sense of drama, a belief that they were taking a step that would transform their lives. On the sides of train cars migrants chalked signs proclaiming "Bound for the Promised Land" or "Bound to the Land

The first lodge of black Masons was founded in 1787. By the early 20th century, membership in the Masons and similar organizations helped African Americans build local and regional networks. National conventions permitted even broader contact.

of Hope." A teenager relocating to Detroit from southwest Tennessee expected to see the Mason-Dixon line, which he thought would be marked by a row of trees. It was not. But when he learned that he had crossed the famous line of demarcation that had once separated slave from free, he walked out of the Jim Crow car and searched for an empty seat next to a white passenger. A woman from Hattiesburg, Mississippi, later claimed that when her train crossed the Ohio River the air felt "lighter," permitting her to breathe more easily.

Black men served as waiters, cooks, and porters on the Pullman trains that crossed the country.

Alighting in a train depot downtown could stimulate comparable exhilaration, which writer Richard Wright recalled feeling when he looked around the station for the familiar "FOR WHITE" and "FOR COLORED" signs that hung over water fountains, bathrooms, snack bars, and elsewhere in Southern terminals. He paused at a newsstand, feeling a tinge of anxiety as he exchanged coin for newspaper, "without having to wait until a white man was served."

Martel Meriweather similarly recalled her move from Texas to San Francisco during World War I: "It was just like coming from hell to heaven. . . . [Children] could run up and down the streets and play and they wasn't called nigger and all this kind of stuff. And they wasn't denied the privilege to play in front of white people's yards and so on like that. And I love that. I love that freedom."

For some, this sense of liberation was tempered by a combination of uncertainty, anxiety, and even fear. One newcomer recalled feeling "completely lost. . . . I was afraid to ask anyone where to go." The famed musician Louis Armstrong later recalled his terror upon disembarking in a Chicago train station in 1922. He scanned the crowd, unable to locate his mentor Joe Oliver, who had made the same journey from New Orleans a few years earlier:

> I saw a million people, but not Mister Joe, and I didn't give a damn who else
> was there. I never seen a city that big. All those tall buildings. I thought they

were universities. I said, no, this is the wrong city. I was fixing to take the next train back home—standing there in my box-back suit, padded shoulders, double-breasted wide-leg pants.

Armstrong's anxiety, one that characterized millions of immigrants to American cities decades before and after he made his move, was very different from Wright's. Armstrong worried about city life. Wright pondered the difficulty of making the transition from a region where the rules of interaction (and separation) were spelled out and inflexible to the more ambiguous patterns of the North.

He would have been even more anxious had he been aware of the experience of another future literary giant, Langston Hughes, who had naively crossed the "dead line" on Chicago's South Side soon after his arrival in 1918. The unfortunate youth had wandered onto Irish gang turf and was promptly set upon and beaten.

Upon arrival, however, few black Southerners were thinking about the dangers of their new environments. Rudolph Fisher, in his short story "City of Refuge," captures the sense of liberation and expectation that characterized the first moments. His protagonist, King Solomon Gillis, has just arrived in New York and is emerging from the subway at the corner of Lenox Avenue and 135th Street in Harlem:

> Casting about for direction, the tall newcomer's glance caught inevitably on the most conspicuous thing in sight, a magnificent figure in blue that stood in the middle of the crossing and blew a whistle and waved great white-gloved hands. The Southern Negro's eyes opened wide; his mouth opened wider. If the inside of New York had mystified him, the outside was amazing him. For there stood a handsome, brass-buttoned giant directing the heaviest traffic Gillis had ever seen; halting unnumbered tons of automobiles and trucks and wagons and pushcarts and street-cars; holding them at bay with one hand while he swept similar tons peremptorily on with the other; ruling the wide crossing with supreme self-assurance; and he, too, was a Negro!
>
> Yet most of the vehicles that leaped or crouched at his bidding carried white passengers. One of these overdrove bounds a few feet and Gillis heard the officer's shrill whistle and gruff reproof, saw the driver's face turn red and his car draw back like a threatened pup. It was beyond belief—impossible.

A BASIC NEED

The Negro needs JOBS—and he needs to know how to keep them.

Efforts to improve the status of the Negro in America will remain superficial until we successfully attack the basic difficulty—lack of sufficient income. Programs for better health, for more recreational and leisure time facilities, for improved home and neighborhood conditions, for higher moral standards are abortive, so long as the pay envelope is empty or only partially filled.

To buy good and proper food, to rent decent homes, to secure adequate education and recreation, the race must first secure JOBS.

The color of one's skin is no indication of ability or lack of it, and should not be a factor in employment. The Negro has a right to look for a job wherever he has the ability to perform the task specified. Particularly has he the right to look to those who cater to his trade for an opportunity to earn a living.

BUT the Negro must also learn how to hold the jobs he now has. He must display the qualities that will make him valuable on the job, which he hopes to get. No verbal plea for erasing the color line in industry will ever be as effective as demonstrated efficiency, reliability, punctuality, and honesty on the job.

To get a job, to hold it, and to secure a better job, the Negro must examine himself, study his weaknesses, secure training and give—a day's work for a day's pay.

R. MAURICE MOSS.

DISTRIBUTED BY THE LOUISVILLE URBAN LEAGUE.

CHAPTER 6

THE PROMISE OF THE CITIES
◇ ◇ ◇

The Thomas family arrived in Chicago in the spring of 1917. Like thousands of other black Southerners moving north at the time, their first task was to find a home. For a week they pounded the pavements of the South Side ghetto. To look elsewhere would have been futile. In Chicago the "black belt," along with a few other scattered neighborhoods, provided the only housing available to African Americans. The parents, their 19-year-old daughter, and a son two years younger crowded into a five-room apartment—cramped, but probably larger than the farmhouse they had left behind in Alabama.

The second task was to find work. The men went off to the stockyards; the women turned to the familiar trade of wringing the dirt out of other people's clothing. Optimistic about the future, the teenagers spent their evenings in night school, hoping to improve on the grade-school education they had brought with them from a rural Southern schoolhouse. In their free time the family explored the leisure activities available on Chicago's South Side, carrying picnics into the park and venturing into theaters and ice-cream parlors.

This family's experience hardly invokes the idea of a "Second Emancipation." Yet its ordinary story tells as much about the Great Migration as the dramatic recollections of migrants who looked out of train windows and saw black southerners arrested as "vagrants" at Southern train stations, or the families who sang songs of deliverance as they crossed the Ohio River.

The National Urban League struggled to get black workers promoted into skilled jobs. To support its efforts, it stressed the importance of education and self-help.

The Thomases struggled with the mundane aspects of everyday life that confront anyone who leaves home to begin a new life elsewhere. For poor people this was a particularly daunting challenge. For African Americans in the first half of the 20th century, most choices also were limited by racial discrimination. By 1918 migration chains linking South and North enabled thousands of Southerners to choose destinations where they had friends or relatives to offer a welcoming hand. A Southern town, city, or county might develop links to many Northern cities, but a particularly strong connection usually reached toward one or two potential destinations.

A native of Abbeville, South Carolina, for example, could move to Philadelphia without worrying about where she might sleep the first night in town. From Hattiesburg, Mississippi, a newcomer could easily find the Hattiesburg Barber Shop in Chicago and be directed to the appropriate boardinghouse.

In most cases these patterns conformed to lines of longitude, largely because of railroad routes. North and South Carolinians went to New York, Philadelphia, and other eastern seaboard cities. Pittsburgh's African-American newcomers were likely to hail from Alabama, Georgia, or Kentucky. From Mississippi, Louisiana, Tennessee, and parts of Georgia and Alabama, people headed for Chicago—an especially popular destination because of the influence of the *Chicago Defender* and the long tentacles of the Illinois Central Railroad.

With these connections established it was not difficult to make arrangements before leaving home. "Let me know what day you expect to leave and over what road, and if I don't meet you I will have some one there to meet you and look after you until I see you," one woman wrote from Chicago to a member of her former church in Mississippi. These kinds of community and family contacts had tied Southern cities to their hinterlands for decades; they now extended north. A thin strand even stretched westward from Texas and Oklahoma, laying the foundation for more significant growth of black communities in West Coast cities during World War II.

Arriving during a wartime housing shortage, most migrants encountered difficulty finding a home. Choices were limited. In the largest cities, emerging African-American ghettos provided obvious starting points, with New York's Harlem and Chicago's South Side especially well known among Southerners. In medium-sized cities like Cleveland, Milwaukee, and Buffalo, the process of ghettoization had begun before the Great Migration, but there was not yet a district so dominated by black residents that the neighborhood seemed segregated. In Los Angeles most blacks

---

If You are a Stranger in the City

If you want a job   If you want a place to live
If you are having trouble with your employer
If you want information or advice of any kind

CALL UPON

The CHICAGO LEAGUE ON URBAN CONDITIONS AMONG NEGROES

3719 South State Street

Telephone Douglas 9098   T. ARNOLD HILL, Executive Secretary

No charges—no fees. We want to help YOU

---

lived in an area that stretched 30 blocks along Central Avenue, but as late as 1919 their neighbors included Mexicans, Italians, and Russian Jews.

In some cases local geography was a crucial factor. Pittsburgh's hills and hollows, breaking towards the rivers, contrasted sharply with Chicago's flat prairie or the unbroken expanse of Manhattan Island. African-American steelworkers in the Pittsburgh area did not inhabit a single district, instead congregating in a series of steel mill communities with the largest concentration in Pittsburgh itself. Still, however, they tended to live in enclaves, in neighborhoods that became increasingly segregated during World War I and the 1920s.

In general northbound migrants entered cities where housing segregation had proceeded far enough to exclude them from most neighborhoods. But the state of flux was such that in most cases a black Northerner in 1920 was likely to have at least a few white neighbors within a couple of blocks. By 1930, that likelihood had diminished considerably, with African Americans segregated into ghettos—neighborhoods dominated by a single group excluded from other parts of the city.

Ghettos are not, however, necessarily slums. Harlem, in particular, was not a slum on the eve of the Great Migration. A middle-class neighborhood barely a decade earlier, it suffered from overcrowding during and after the war. Most urban black neighborhoods were less fortunate at the outset, with aging housing stock ill suited to the rapid influx of newcomers beginning in 1916.

Segregation by itself did not cause a decline in either housing standards or the quality of a neighborhood. What segregation meant was that

The migration to Chicago peaked in 1923. After arrival most migrants generally headed straight for established black neighborhoods, such as New York's Harlem and Chicago's South Side.

neither black newcomers nor established residents could move beyond the borders of the emerging ghettos, except for gradual expansion at the fringes of these neighborhoods. The result was overcrowding and a strain on the physical capacity of buildings.

This strain was also a result of the economics of ghettoization. Contrary to popular belief, property values have not always declined as neighborhoods shifted from "white" to "black." During the Great Migration and throughout much of the 20th century the process was more complicated. As Southerners, most of them poor and unaccustomed to urban life, moved into the least expensive and oldest neighborhoods, established residents tended to seek better housing in less crowded districts. But ghettos could expand only slowly, and only at their edges. Real estate speculators purchased homes in these border districts, often by frightening white homeowners with the prospect of "Negro invasion." Known as "blockbusting," this tactic yielded generous profits, as the investor could sell the properties to black home buyers at inflated rates. In Los Angeles, for example the markup (in essence a race tax) went as high as 100 percent. African-American purchasers had nowhere else to go because of the limitations defined by a dual housing market: one set of choices for whites, one (more limited) for blacks. In Northern and Western cities, African Americans generally paid more than whites would pay for equivalent living space.

At the same time, however, black workers earned less than their white counterparts. What this meant was that African Americans spent an inordinate proportion of their income on shelter. In Harlem, rents generally commanded nearly half of the earnings of African-American residents, placing a considerable burden on family budgets. There and elsewhere, the solution often lay in transforming a home into a commercial enterprise. Families rented out rooms to lodgers, often relatives or former neighbors recently arrived from the South.

Lodging, however, constituted only one type of residential over-crowding. In the long run, the deterioration of buildings probably owed more to a different way of crowding more people into limited spaces—the division of houses and apartments into smaller units by landlords eager to squeeze out more rent. Real estate investors who operated in the "white" market made profits by developing what are known as "subdivisions," large tracts of land divided into individual lots for residential construction. Building a subdivision increased the value of the land and its environs.

Rickety back porches supported clotheslines in this Cincinnati tenement.

On the African-American side of the dual housing market, a very different kind of "subdivision" took place, one that was equally profitable but that eventually drove values down rather than up. An investor would purchase a single-family home or an apartment building and divide the structure into a rabbit warren of small apartments, known in some cities as "kitchenettes" and in others as "efficiency units." These spaces were efficient because their inhabitants (often families) slept, cooked, ate, socialized, and relaxed in a single room. The rental income from these converted buildings yielded a quick profit, thereby increasing the value of the property. But these buildings deteriorated equally rapidly, due to shoddy renovation and inadequate maintenance.

The dual housing market contributed to the deterioration of some African-American neighborhoods in other ways as well. With a captive market for their properties, landlords collected rents more assiduously than they maintained their buildings. Tenants who demanded proper maintenance (and many of them did) could usually be replaced with newcomers who either knew little about what to expect or took what they could get because choices were few.

African Americans who purchased homes often overpaid because of their inability to shop throughout the city. In some cases this left homeowners without enough money to maintain their houses adequately.

Living conditions in the tenements were grim. There was little indoor plumbing, and residents made do with basins and chamber pots. In most cases, however, even these homes were better than what was available in the South.

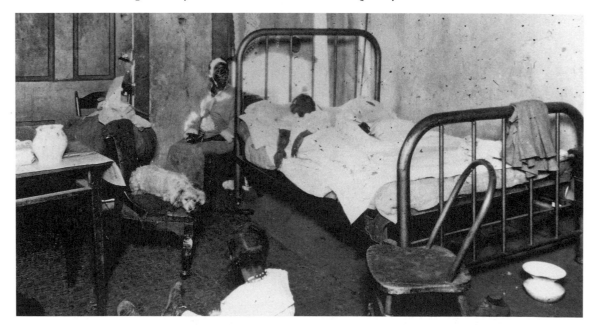

Despite the continuing presence of middle-class African-American neigh-borhoods, invisible to whites who blithely equated slum with ghetto, the trend was downward.

During World War I and sporadically during the 1920s it was easier for black newcomers to find places to work in Northern cities than to find places to live. The Great Migration itself was catalyzed by the opening of thousands of new railroad jobs, mainly laying track and performing manual tasks around rail yards. By 1917, although still largely excluded from indus-trial work in the West, African Americans were working in heavy industry across the Northeast and Midwest.

On the whole these black men and women were relegated to jobs disdained by their white counterparts, who took advantage of wartime opportunities to advance into more skilled positions. As one Milwaukee steelworker put it, jobs for black men "were limited, they only did the dirty work . . . jobs that even Poles didn't want."

Most of these jobs in steel mills, auto plants, packinghouses, and rubber factories required little skill and could be learned quickly. The hardest part for many migrants from the South was probably the adaptation to a different approach to time—an adjustment confronted by generations of rural workers around the world upon their introduction to industrial employment.

In the rural South, as in other agricultural societies, the calendar and the weather determined the rhythm of work. Planting, cultivating, and har-vesting were performed at the same time each year, but with variation according to the weather. Cotton cultivation was characterized by one planter as "a series of spurts rather than by a daily grind." A woman picking cotton could arrive in the fields ten minutes late with no penalty other than a slightly reduced output for the day. Where workers did have to sustain a regular pace in the South—hired labor on some plantations, railroad-tie layers, dockhands, construction gangs, sawmill laborers, and turpentine crews—a work song set the rhythm. Men laying railroad ties set a cadence to their efforts with songs like "Raise the Iron":

> Down the railroad, um-huh
> Well, raise the iron, um-huh
> Raise the iron, um-huh

These songs were flexible. The pace could be changed by the song leader, who set the tempo. Jazzman Big Bill Broonzy recalled that during his days laying railroad ties in Mississippi between 1912 and 1915, a man who wished to relieve himself would signal the leader, who would "sing it to the boss." Upon the boss's nod, he would sing, "Everybody lay their bar down, it's one to go." When the worker returned from the bushes the leader would start the crew up again with "All men to their places like horses to their traces."

This would not work on an assembly line in Detroit. By the early 20th century, workers in most Northern factories were punching time clocks. Arrive ten minutes late and your pay was docked one hour. On the "disassembly lines" of the packinghouses, conveyer belts moved carcasses from worker to worker, each of whom would make a single cut. Tardiness or absence could disrupt the whole process. Moreover, once the line began moving the newcomer had no control over the pace of work.

In agricultural work and rural industry the only way a supervisor could force an employee to work faster was to cajole or threaten; in the packinghouses, noted an executive at Swift & Company, "If you need to turn out a little more you speed up the conveyers a little and the men speed up to keep pace." The demand for work itself was unpredictable, determined by the seasonal fluctuation or production decisions made by managers.

Steelworkers in Missouri. During World War I, immigration of Europeans stopped, opening new opportunities for African Americans to work in factories.

Newcomers to industrial labor also had to accustom themselves to repeating a single task rather than completing an operation from start to finish. A man who formerly butchered a whole hog now performed only a single task among more than a hundred. A woman accustomed to picking up dirty laundry from customers and dropping it off cleaned and ironed might take a job in one of the many mechanized laundries employing thousands of black women in Northern and Southern cities. There she could spend hour after hour, day after day, only pressing cuffs, yokes, or sleeves.

What did not require adjustment was hard work. "I will & can do eny kind of worke," declared one man just before heading north from his Florida home. Men with farm experience—even migrants from towns and cities tended to have spent at least part of their life working the land—were accustomed to a workday that began at dawn and ended at sundown. Black women, responsible in both rural and urban settings for household labor as well as producing income, began earlier and ended later. "I came here to Philadelphia because people said it was better," recalled Ella Lee of her early years in that city, "so much better living in the North than it was in the South. But so far as I am concerned you have got to work like a dog to have anything anywhere you go."

The difference for most migrants, the reason why most not only stayed but encouraged their friends and relatives to join them, was that the hard work produced rewards during the war years and the 1920s. In interviews and in letters back home, migrants spoke enthusiastically of sending their children to school, voting, sitting where they pleased on the streetcars, and other accomplishments.

At work, newcomers had little difficulty adapting to industrial time discipline or learning how to perform the tasks required by their new jobs. Although black women in the North were pushed out of industry and into domestic employment after World War I, even domestic service paid better in the North than in the South. Black men retained their industrial footholds. Many moved from unskilled into semiskilled, and occasionally even skilled positions, which put more cash in their pay envelopes and suggested the possibility of further promotion down the road.

Migrants to Southern cities encountered a somewhat different employment picture. With fewer basic manufacturing industries than Northern cities, places like Louisville, Norfolk, Nashville, and Mobile provided fewer opportunities. Industries directly related to war production, especially shipyards in coastal cities, provided most of the new jobs. But where black men in the North generally held onto their foothold at the bottom of the industrial ladder until nearly the end of the 1920s, their Southern counterparts suffered the fate of black women: when the war ended most were pushed back into menial service employment.

Northern employers were willing to permit black industrial workers to keep their positions in part because they had learned during the war that these men could do the job. But the decision drew equally on two other factors: immigration restriction and the threat of unionization. Beginning in 1921 federal legislation limited immigration from nations outside the Western hemisphere to a trickle, once again forcing industrialists to look beyond European immigrants for a supply of new workers.

At the same time, union organizing campaigns in major industries during the war had convinced Northern employers that maintaining racial divisions within their work force was a strong weapon against unionization. When African-American workers passed through factory gates to their new jobs during the war, they had a reputation among white workers and employers as instinctively antiunion. This image was not entirely accurate. Black Southerners had joined unions as early as 1872 on the New Orleans docks. In cities across the South, black carpenters and bricklayers had joined segregated union locals around the turn of the century. Indeed after organizing black brewery workers in New Orleans in 1906–7, one white unionist claimed that "as strikers, there could be no better."

On the whole, however, few black workers did belong to unions, largely because most unions either excluded them from membership or simply made no attempt to organize them. In addition, most unions at the time organized mainly skilled craft workers such as carpenters, bricklayers, plumbers, printers, and cigar makers, showing little interest in the agricultural and service occupations in which most African Americans worked. Only the United Mine Workers (UMW) and the Industrial Workers of the World (IWW) systematically organized unskilled workers.

The IWW had little presence in areas populated by African Americans, although it did have some success among black dockworkers in Philadelphia and timber workers in the Louisiana forests. The UMW stood alone among major national unions in its willingness and ability to enlist African-American members. But even among the mine workers, racial divisions frequently hampered the ability of the union to maintain solidarity. Thus when white union workers went on strike, employers could—and occasionally did—tap a substantial pool of underemployed and nonunion

ALL APPLICATIONS for MEMBERSHIP CAN BE MADE AT THE FOLLOWING PLACES
GRZIE MOŻNA SIE ZAPISAC DO UNII
COLUMBIA HALL   MICKIECZ HALL   McDERMOTTS HALL   LOCAL 651
                                                    HEADQUARTERS
PULAWSKI HALL   LOCAL 212   4300 STATE ST.
COME IN NOW WHILE THE ADMISSION FEE IS SMALL. PAY UP YOUR DUES
WEAR A CAMPAIGN BUTTON SO AS WE WILL KNOW WHO IS UNION & WHO IS NOT.

Labor unions recruited both black and white stockyard workers in Chicago. This banner is in both Polish and English. Most unions, however, either excluded African Americans or relegated them to secondary status.

African Americans to replace the strikers. In coal mines and packinghouses, on the railroads and in hotel restaurants, African-American workers had filled the places of white unionists on strike since the closing decades of the 19th century.

Between 1917 and 1921, unions undertook major organizing campaigns most notably (in terms of the role of black workers) in steel, meat packing, and coal. Except in the Appalachian coal mines these campaigns made little headway in the South, but in major industrial centers across the Northeast and Midwest workers joined by the thousands. What made a difference was that for the first time, unions in steel and meat packing organized by *industry,* as coal miners did, rather than by *craft,* or specific occupation, as workers did in the building trades. In addition union leadership recognized that black workers were now part of the industrial labor force and would have to be included if an organizing campaign were to succeed.

Many black industrial workers did join unions during and immediately after the war, but more either dropped out quickly or never joined at all. Some black workers had difficulty appreciating the sincerity of the unions' welcome, given the record of racial exclusion and the continuing hostility among white workers and local union leadership in some areas. Others were reluctant to risk the jobs that had provided the path out of the Jim Crow South. Perhaps most important, however, was the difference in how black and white workers saw the relationship between their community and their workplace.

White industrial workers often lived in neighborhoods near the plant; unions were as much community institutions as workplace institutions. In most cities, however, African Americans lived in increasingly segregated neighborhoods away from their workplaces, which tended to be lumped with a white world dominated by white institutions.

New York's Harlem and Chicago's South Side ghetto in the 1920s, singer Mahalia Jackson later recalled, were places where "the Negro went

Delegates to the first annual convention of the Brotherhood of Sleeping Car Porters in 1929. A. Philip Randolph is seated second from left in the front row.

home after working to earn his money in other parts of the city. When he got there he could lay down his burden of being a colored person in the white man's world and lead his own life." Here, labeled the "home sphere" by one historian, black workers were more likely to look to black institutions for leadership. Except for the handful of African-American unions, most notably the Brotherhood of Sleeping Car Porters, founded in 1925, unions were likely to be perceived as white organizations, unable or unwilling to understand the needs of black workers.

Even though black workers identified strongly with their community and its institutions, the class differences that preceded the Great Migration remained. Indeed, these Northern urban black communities now experienced even deeper divisions. Newcomers were more likely than established residents to come from the Deep South and to work at industrial jobs that previously had played no role in the black class structure because blacks had been excluded from these workplaces. They also encountered African-American communities that encouraged migration yet held the migrants themselves at arm's length. "They didn't seem to open-arm welcome them," recalled a porter at one of Chicago's busy railroad stations, "but they seemed to welcome them."

People who called themselves "Old Philadelphians" ("O.P.'s") in one city, or "Old Settlers" in others, generally considered northbound migration to be "good for the race." The wages workers carried home increased the flow of dollars into black businesses. The votes of newcomers, most of them loyal to the Republican party, increased the clout of black politicians. Moreover their departure from the South dealt a blow to Jim Crow and proclaimed to the nation that black Southerners were not the "happy negroes" depicted by Southern white spokesmen. The Cleveland *Gazette*, echoing other African-American newspapers, cheered the exodus as evidence that black Southerners understood the folly of "depending upon the people [white southerners] who have destroyed them in the past to aid them in the future." Instead, migrants could depend on black leadership in Northern communities to represent their interests and ease the transition to their new homes.

Black Southerners arriving in cities encountered an array of agencies committed to helping them find places in the city. The most systematically active and professionalized of these were the local branches of the National Urban League. Founded in 1911, the Urban League added dozens of branches during the decade after 1916, in a wide variety of cities across the country.

Although services varied from city to city, the Urban League developed a reputation among black Southerners preparing to leave home as an organization "that cares for Southern emigrants." This care came in the form of job and housing registries, which often dispensed advice on work habits, housekeeping, and coping with landlords and city officials. Urban League officials in Pittsburgh proudly referred to their instructions to women on "the use of gas, electricity, marketing of foods, how to purchase and prepare cheap cuts of meat."

Black branches of the Young Men's and Young Women's Christian Associations initiated cooperative programs with employers and established room registries and recreation programs. In some cases community centers, churches, and women's clubs developed day care programs, a crucial service given the unusually high level of married African-American women who held paid jobs. The husbands of black working women earned less than white men. Thus it was not unusual for these women to add wage labor to the customary housekeeping burdens of wives and mothers.

In 1919, the Urban League of Pittsburgh ran its second annual Negro Health Education Campaign. It advised African Americans to seek medical attention for infectious diseases, to see their dentists regularly, and to practice good sanitation.

The assistance of clubs and groups like the Urban League, however, came with a double edge. Clubwomen concerned about the availability of child care for domestic workers were equally concerned about respectable housekeeping habits and public appearance. Newcomers were told not to wear head rags, scarves that Northern black women saw as symbols of servility and second-class citizenship. On a front porch shoes were a must, aprons a no-no. Like the settlement houses in white immigrant neighborhoods, YMCAs and YWCAs tried to compete with the streets and saloons for workers' leisure hours. And like the settlement houses, their efforts, though well meant, were often insulting and only partly successful.

Black newspapers printed lists of "do's and don'ts" similar to the lectures printed on Urban League brochures. Most

The future of the Negro lies in his Health.

WAR, DISEASE, FAMINE Now a MEMORY

Reconstruction in 1919 must begin with toning up the health of the individual and comunity.

The War's backwash caused Pittsburgh's death rate to increase 43% last year.

Negroes suffered greatly. The amount of sickness was appalling.

7,320 deaths in Pittsburgh from **Pneumonia** and **Influenza** last year. 630 were Negroes.

To YOU, who have recovered, Specialists say that "the after effects are as bad or worse than the disease."

Watch that weakened Heart or those Kidneys or Lungs. If in doubt —see your Doctor.

Tuberculosis kills relatively almost twice as many Negroes as white people;—if treated in time, it can be cured. Consult the Tuberculosis Dispensary at once.

Bad teeth means a bad stomach, which cause indirectly 75% of all sickness.

The Medical examination of our draftees—your sons, husbands and sweethearts has shown the alarming prevalence of Venereal diseases. Read that Literature.

ARE YOU MOVING? READ

A Negro family moved into a house vacated by a foreigner in the East End one month ago. One week afterward the whole family, man, wife and three children were seriously ill from germs left in the house—one child died. "Nuf Sed."

Fully half of all the sickness and deaths are preventable, this means that 45 out of every 100 Negroes who died last year ought to be living.

BABIES DO NOT HAVE TO HAVE Measles, Scarlet Fever, Whooping Cough, etc.

Twice as many Negro babies die before they reach one year of age than babies of all other races in the City.

Find the nearest Baby Health Station and take your baby regularly.

The League Office will give you information on request.

IMMEDIATE STEPS.

See that your garbage and waste is moved promptly.

Don't live in or over damp basements.

of these lessons dealt with public behavior, reflecting anxieties about the impact of the migrants' Southern and rural habits on white images of African Americans. When newcomers were lectured not to "allow children to beg on the streets," encourage gambling, congregate in loud crowds, or "act discourteously to other people in public places," they sensed they were being talked down to. And they were.

In the North, even among African Americans, Southerners encountered a contempt for rural Southern culture. At the same time, however, these instructions reflected realistic concerns about Northern race relations and the differences between North and South. Northern whites did see African-Americans as belonging to a single, unchanging, unified culture. Whatever black Northerners had accomplished in developing a community reputation could crumble under the onslaught of the new images conveyed by newcomers.

W. E. B. Du Bois recognized the dilemma of streetcar behavior in terms of the prevailing etiquette that required a male passenger to offer his seat to a female. This was something that migrants supposedly did not do, reflecting poorly on African-American manners and gentility. Southern black men were not by nature rude, observed Du Bois. But they had learned in the South to avoid interaction with white women. Even eye contact at the wrong time and place could provoke a lynching. Offering a seat to a white woman implied a social grace, a statement of manhood that was acceptable in the South only if accompanied by the kind of shuffle and deference that had no place in the North. Many black men who had recently arrived from the South took the safe—if "discourteous"—route. When a white woman boarded, they averted their glance and kept their seats.

Many newcomers responded to what they considered a cool reception by distancing themselves, especially on Sunday morning. Thousands left the big urban churches they had initially found so exciting and established smaller congregations in storefronts, often sending back home for their minister. Yet they continued to read the local black newspaper and align themselves politically with the established leaders of their communities.

This identification with the community, with the "home sphere," reflected the ways in which African Americans fit into early-20th-century American cities. Where they could (and could not) live related closely to race. Their children sat in classes filled mainly with other black children but with a white teacher standing in front. Whites owned the big stores, blacks, the small shops. And nearly all bosses were white. For white

DAILY BULLETIN
Annual Conference National Urban League
OCTOBER 16 to 19
Thursday Issue, October 18

12:15 L. HOLLINGSWORTH WOOD, President National Urban League, will speak to the Kiwanis Club.

4 to 8 p. m. Reception at Y. W. C. A.

7:45 p. m., Special Music:
Aesthetic Dance, Pupils of Miss Margaret Lane. Miss Ona Miller Briefer, Harpist.
In the Garden .... Schenetze
Spanish Patrol .... Pedeschi
Carnival of Venice ....Chadderton
Selection .... Centennial Four

8:00 p. m. "Health"
Presiding
DR. GEORGE CLEVELAND HALL, Chicago, Il.

"How The Y. W. C. A. Promotes the Health of Our Women and Girls."
MISS EVA D. BOWLES
National Board, Young Women's Christian Association.

"Improvements in Negro Health as Shown by Insurance Records"
C. C. SPAULDING
President North Carolina Mutual Life Insurance Company.

"Methods by Which Children's Health May Be Improved."
MISS GRACE ABBOTT ,
Chief of Children's Bureau, United States Department of Labor, and President of the National Conference of Social Work.

Thursday Discussion closed by
DR. KATHARINE RICHARDSON of Mercy Hospital, Kansas City, Mo.

FRIDAY, OCTOBER 19th

10:00 a. m. "Causes and Effects of the Migration."
PROFESSOR JOHN HOPE,
President Morehouse College, Atlanta, Ga.

CHARLES S. JOHNSON
Director of the Department of Research and Investigations, National Urban League and Editor of "OPPORTUNITY."

MISS JULIA LATHROP
Ex-President of the National Conference of Social Work.

Discussion to be opened by
T. ARNOLD HILL,
Executive Secretary, Chicago Urban League and Western Field Secretary of the National Urban League.

2:00 p. m. "A Social Program to Help The Migrant."
Presiding
WILLIAM H. BALDWIN,
Treasurer of the Brooklyn (N. Y.) Urban League.

JOHN C. DANCY,
Executive Secretary, Detroit Urban League.

"A Better Health Program"
JAMES H. HUBERT
Executive Secretary, New York Urban League.

"How the Church Can Help"
DR. W. A. C. HUGHES
Bureau of Negro Work, Board of Home Missions of the Methodist Episcopal Church.

Dicussion opened by
JESSE O. THOMAS
Southern Field Secretary of the National Urban League.

8:00 p. m. "Cooperation Between The Church and Social Agencies"
Presiding
THE REV. A. A. GRAHAM
Corresponding Secretary, Lott Carey Baptist Foreign Mission Convention

THE REV. ROBERT NELSON SPENCER, Rector
Grace Holy Trinity Episcopal Church, Kansas City, Mo.

J. R. E. LEE
Extension Secretary, National Urban League

THE REV. ELBERT W. MOORE
Director of Negro Work in the North American Baptist Home Mission Society.

SATURDAY, OCTOBER 20th

10:00 a. m., Sharp—Dr. Howard M. Smith has arranged cars to take all visitors to the County Home for Old Folks and also the County Home for Delinquent Boys. Assemble at Y. M. C. A. at 9:45.

ADDITIONAL WHO'S HERE

MRS. WENDELL GREEN,
Attending Graduate School of Sociology, Chicago.

MONROE N. WORK,
Editor Year Book, Tuskegee Institute, Ala.

DR. W. A. C. HUGHES,
Director Negro Work A.M.E. Church Extension Bureau, Philadelphia, Pa.

ERNEST T. ATWELL,
Field Director Colored Work, Playground and Recreation Association of America, Philadelphia, Pa.

T. M. CAMPBELL,
U. S. Department of Agriculture, Tuskegee, Institute, Tuskegee, Ala.

MISS GRACE ABBOTT,
Chief of Children's Bureau U. S. Department of Labor and President of National Conference of Social Work.

MISS MARTHA T. SPEAKMAN,
Recreation Specialist, Children's Bureau, U. S. Department of Labor.

PLACEMENT SECRETARY WANTED BY CHICAGO URBAN LEAGUE

The National Urban League held its 1923 annual meeting in Kansas City. Among the speakers were John Hope, president of Morehouse College, and Grace Abbott, chief of the Children's Bureau of the U.S. Department of Labor.

workers, race was taken for granted and class divisions often seemed to explain injustices and inequalities. But for black workers—and most African Americans earned working-class incomes—injustice and inequality had a distinctly racial cast. Class differences mattered, especially when thinking about the internal workings of their own community. But "their own community" was defined mainly by race.

Black Southerners who moved north hoping to leave behind the color line and racial hostilities quickly learned a harsher reality. The rules were unwritten in the North, but they were rules nevertheless. These neighborhoods were off-limits; those restaurants "don't serve Negroes." Sit where you want on the streetcar but don't be surprised if a white passenger moves away. Many teachers made no secret of their belief in the inability of black children to learn as quickly as their white peers. And there was violence.

In 1917, less than a year after industrial jobs first opened in the North, black workers in East St. Louis, Illinois (across the Mississippi River from St. Louis, Missouri), learned how dangerous their new homes could be. Thousands of black Southerners had come to work in aluminum factories, many of them recruited by employers seeking to replace striking white workers. The combination was explosive: cynical industrial managers using race to divide their workers, union organizers who raised the familiar cry of "nigger scab," corrupt white politicians, irresponsible journalists, and police inclined to look the other way when whites attacked blacks. The result was a race riot.

Nine whites and at least thirty-nine African Americans were killed; it was impossible to establish the number of black victims because their dead bodies were allegedly thrown into ditches and never recovered. The coroner was more concerned with white fatalities. Thousands of black residents were left homeless by fires set by white arsonists. Three weeks later, Du Bois, James Weldon Johnson, and other NAACP officials led a protest march down New York's Fifth Avenue. Following muffled drums, 10,000 men and women marched from Harlem through the heart of Manhattan in complete silence, with only their signs expressing their outrage.

Two years later violence erupted once more, this time in twenty-five cities and towns during a six-month period. James Weldon Johnson called it the "Red Summer," referring to the blood that flowed from racial conflict. Attacks occurred in rural Arkansas; small-town Texas; Tulsa, Oklahoma;

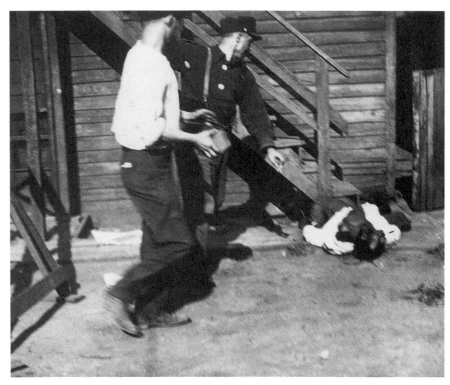

A black man is stoned to death during the Chicago race riot of 1919. When the violence ended, 23 blacks were killed and 342 wounded.

Charleston, South Carolina; Knoxville, Tennessee; Washington, D.C.; and Omaha, Nebraska. Only the West was spared, probably because black populations were not yet large enough to pose a threat to the stability of white neighborhoods or to white men's jobs.

The worst riot was in Chicago, where black and white Chicagoans battled in the streets for five days in July, with occasional attacks punctuating an uneasy calm the following week. Catalyzed by an attack on a black teenager who had floated onto a "white" beach, the violence was initiated by white street gangs fighting to secure their turf, their community's jobs, and their political patrons' power against the threat posed by the influx of African Americans into the city. The police stood by as blacks passing through white neighborhoods were beaten. In response black Chicagoans set upon whites as well, usually inside the boundaries of the black ghetto. Only a timely rainstorm and the Illinois National Guard restored order.

No silent marches this time. In many of these conflicts the protest had come immediately and on the field of battle. Nineteenth-century "race riots" had generally consisted of attacks on black communities, comparable to the pogroms that drove thousands of Jews from their homes in Russia

A triumphant group of young rioters celebrate outside a damaged home during the 1919 Chicago riots.

and Poland while authorities looked the other way. Blacks sometimes defended themselves but seldom counterattacked. But in Longview, Texas, in 1919, blacks responded to an attempt to drive the local *Defender* agent out of town by taking out their rifles. In Chicago white peddlers and merchants in the "Black Belt" were attacked after the initial assaults on African Americans. Claude McKay's poem, *If We Must Die,* published in July 1919, articulated the mood:

If we must die, let it not be like hogs
Hunted and penned in an inglorious spot,
While round us bark the mad and hungry dogs,
Making their mock at our accursed lot.
If we must die, O let us nobly die,
So that our precious blood may not be shed
In vain; then even the monsters we defy
Shall be constrained to honor us though dead!
O kinsmen! we must meet the common foe!
Though far outnumbered let us show us brave,
And for their thousand blows deal one deathblow!
What though before us lies the open grave?
Like men we'll face the murderous, cowardly pack,
Pressed to the wall, dying, but fighting back!

CHAPTER 7

"NEW NEGROES"

On February 17, 1919, less than two years after the dramatic "silent protest" parade from Harlem to downtown Manhattan, another set of disciplined marchers walked Fifth Avenue in the opposite direction. The men of the 369th Infantry Division of the United States Army had returned home from the war. They had fought hard, losing hundreds of men on the battlefield. They had fought well, becoming the only American unit to win the prized Croix de Guerre from the French, who had dubbed the unit the "Hell Fighters."

The French knew these Americans well, because the regiment had been attached to the French Army—"owing to the need for replacements in French units," according to U.S. government documents prepared after the war. The truth, however, was more complicated. Four National Guard units fought with the French. The troops were black; the officers an interracial group headed in three cases by a white colonel. Only the Illinois regiment, the pride of African Americans across the United States because of publicity from the *Chicago Defender,* had an African American in command.

Combining these regiments with white units was unthinkable to American military leaders. Nor were these generals prepared to combine the African-American units into a fully-equipped all-black combat division. With the French clamoring for replacements, American commanders loaned to their allies the men they preferred not to lead into battle themselves. Appropriately, the war heroes stepped uptown in American uniforms but in French drill formation.

The decision of the United States government to enter World War I in April 1917 received a mixed reception among the American public.

The 302nd Stevedore Regiment lines up for mess at an army camp in France. Most blacks served in service units and labor battalions, where they did manual or relatively unskilled jobs.

131

Many Americans opposed participation. Ethnic loyalties played a part in this opposition, as did criticism of European imperialism and a sense that Europe's troubles need not consume American lives or tax dollars. Many African Americans, questioning their role in a "white-folks' war," shared this skepticism. Asked if he planned to enlist, one Harlem resident observed cynically that "Germans ain't done *nuthin'* to me, and if they have I forgive 'em." Most black voices, however, supported W. E. B. Du Bois's call for African Americans to "close ranks" behind the war effort. Military service, Liberty Bond purchases, diligent labor on the home front, and vocal support for the war would provide a basis upon which the black community could expect increased recognition and acceptance. As one black teacher in the South explained, his people were "soldiers of freedom. . . . When we have proved ourselves men, worthy to work and fight and die for our country, a grateful nation may gladly give us the recognition of real men, and the rights and privileges of true and loyal citizens of these United States." Democracy at home would be the reward for supporting democracy abroad.

The American military, however, had difficulty determining a potential role for black soldiers. First the army turned away black candidates for enlistment. Next, draft boards discriminated against black men seeking exemption. Grudgingly the War Department established a facility to train black officers, but the selection process weeded out many of the most qualified candidates in favor of men less likely to succeed. Black soldiers were

Members of the 369th Colored Infantry arrive home in New York in 1919. Every member of this unit—the first of the African-American troops to see action—received the Croix de Guerre for gallantry.

"loaned" to the French army, whose officers were warned by American authorities that such men were potential rapists who had to be kept away from civilian populations.

In the end, 380,000 black men served, nearly half of them in Europe. Only 42,000 of these served in combat units. The rest were relegated to digging, cleaning, hauling, loading, and unloading. In many ways Ellen Tarry's recollection of the home front in Birmingham, Alabama, described the tenor of black military service as well: "Though we carried huge signs in the parade about fighting for democracy and how everybody should buy bonds, the Negro children were still put at the end of the procession."

Despite these efforts to insult black soldiers and to remind black civilians that a war fought to "make the world safe for Democracy," as President Woodrow Wilson put it, did not necessarily mean making America itself any more democratic, African Americans drew their own lessons from the war. Writing in *The Crisis* in May 1919, Du Bois made the point:

> We *return*
> We *return from fighting.*
> We *return fighting.*
> Make way for Democracy! We saved it in France, and by the Great Jehovah, we will save it in the United States of America or know the reason why.

White Southerners wasted little time casting doubt on whether democracy had been saved at home. They lynched 70 African Americans

African-American women in Newark, New Jersey, ran this club for servicemen during World War I. Black communities were also active in selling bonds to support the war effort.

during the year after the war. Ten of these were soldiers, some murdered in their uniforms. The riots of 1919 both punctuated this epidemic of publicly sanctioned homicide and dispelled any notions that racism and violence were unique to the South.

The riots also, however, provided a clue to an increasingly assertive sensibility spreading across black America. In some Southern cities the violence itself was sparked by white outrage at the sight of armed black veterans in uniform. In the North the riots were linked to the impact of the Great Migration, itself a statement of bold ambition and a commitment to a new role in American life. Everywhere the heightened tensions were related to an impatient mood working its way across black America. Black soldiers epitomized this sense of anticipation, this expectation that things were changing, that things had to change. Men who had fought for their country abroad had little tolerance for continued appeals to "wait" for recognition of their rights as citizens at home. This sense that they were entitled to the full rewards of American life combined with the ambition and excitement of the Great Migration to form the heart of what came to be called the "New Negro" movement.

The idea of the "New Negro" took hold in many influential black publications in the 1920s, and the term itself was used as the title of a book edited by Howard University professor Alain Locke in 1925. In his introduction Locke proposed two complementary principles underlying this new perspective. New Negroes insisted on the rights embodied in "the ideals of American institutions and democracy." They also promoted "self-respect and self-reliance" among African Americans, with a distinct emphasis on race pride.

This perspective was not as new as Locke claimed. Instead it brought together strands of Booker T. Washington's gospel of self-reliance, deep traditions of African-American protest, ranging from abolitionism to the founding of the NAACP in 1910, and the hopes and aspirations underlying the Great Migration. What was new was a sense of expectation unequaled since emancipation and an odd combination of disillusionment, anger, militancy, and euphoria dramatized by the parades of returning veterans.

Nor was the New Negro represented by a single approach to African-American culture or the problems defined by the American color line. New Negroes moved into the arts and literature, social work and social activism, politics, the union movement, and a variety of organizations claiming to offer the solution to the dilemma of black life in a nation seemingly committed to white supremacy.

The most enduring expression of the New Negro was the literary and artistic flowering often referred to as the Harlem Renaissance. The term encompasses the work of a broad variety of novelists, poets, essayists, artists, and musicians. Their work displayed a diversity of form and content that defies simple categorization. Some, like poet Langston Hughes and folklorist and novelist Zora Neale Hurston, took street life or rural folk culture as their subject. This approach differed from older African-American literary traditions, which tended to emphasize respectability. Trained in cultural anthropology at Columbia University, Hurston spent much of her life collecting folklore in the rural South. Her novels drew on this fieldwork, along with her recollections of the scene from the front porch of the general store in her native Eatonville, Florida—the setting for *Their Eyes Were Watching God* and *Jonah's Gourd Vine*.

Others, like novelist Jessie Fauset, stuck with high culture and the black elite. Some explicitly protested against American racial oppression; others adopted racial themes but avoided overt political statements. What mattered, declared Hughes, was the inclination to write from inside the experience and to be true to one's creative muse:

> We younger Negro artists who create now intend to express our individual dark-skinned selves without fear or shame. If white people are pleased we are glad. If they are not, it doesn't matter. We know we are beautiful. And ugly too. The tom-tom cries and the tom-tom laughs. If colored people are pleased we are glad. If they are not, their displeasure doesn't matter. We build our temples for tomorrow, strong as we know how, and we stand on the top of the mountain, free within ourselves.

To Fauset that freedom had a social purpose as well, because it would enable the production of more honest (and therefore less exotic) images of African-American people and communities. "The portrayal of black people," she argued, "calls increasingly for black writers."

By the 1920s Harlem had emerged as the cultural capital of black America, in much the same way that New York City stood at the center of mainstream American high culture. This was not an accident. The diversity of the population—a yeasty mix of New Yorkers, recent migrants from the South, and immigrants from the West Indies and Africa—played a part.

So did the efforts of Charles Johnson, an African-American sociologist who at the time was the editor of the Urban League publication *Opportunity*. Johnson, along with *Crisis* literary editor

Folklorist and writer Zora Neale Hurston combined her academic training in anthropology with a keen ear for the voices of rural African Americans.

Jessie Fauset, envisioned their journals as vanguards of social change. Through the publication of short stories, poems, and essays, and the awarding of cash prizes, these two journals promoted the work of Hughes, Hurston, Countee Cullen, Jean Toomer, and countless others. Perhaps as important, the journals also provided a bridge across which African-American culture could be presented to white audiences.

And indeed, white Americans did discover African-American culture during the 1920s. A small group of white political activists, literary figures, editors, and intellectuals read the books, went to art exhibits, and even donated money for literary prizes. Few tackled the more difficult work, like Toomer's *Cane,* a series of fictional portraits connected by poetic interludes. But then again, few blacks read *Cane* either; it sold only 500 copies. Toomer's deft manipulation of literary form to explore the rural roots of black culture and consciousness would become a classic, but it would take nearly a half-century for it to be rediscovered.

Jessie Fauset's genteel aristocrats, every bit as proper as their white counterparts but not nearly as affluent, posed a different challenge. "White readers just don't expect Negroes to be like this," explained one white editor in rejecting her manuscript. The street hustlers of Claude McKay's *Home to Harlem,* the love poems of Countee Cullen, the blues rhythms of Langston Hughes: these were easier. Charles Johnson's vision of a cultural terrain that provided a common ground for black and white Americans overestimated the interest of whites in black culture, history, or sensibilities. Whites were mainly interested in something called "The Negro," an exotic neighbor who was not bound by the narrow conventions of social morality.

It was not the literature or the art that brought white people and their money to Harlem or the South Side of Chicago. It was the nightclubs. White urbanites crowded into the clubs to listen to a new kind of music called jazz, which had emerged in the South earlier in the century. Some of these night spots, owned and operated by whites, employed black

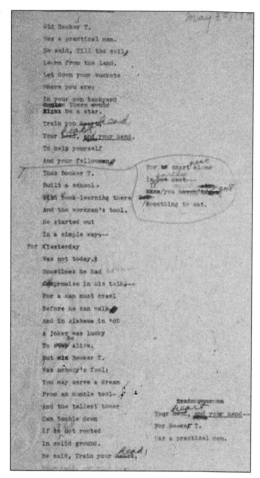

The first draft of Langston Hughes's poem "The Ballad of Booker T."

musicians and chorus girls to entertain mainly white audiences who saw Harlem and its smaller counterparts in other cities as places where they could cast aside their inhibitions and enjoy exotic entertainment. Other clubs resembled Chicago's "black and tan" cabarets, where the white downtown theater crowd mingled with the black middle class. In some cities these integrated establishments were the most likely night spots to attract police in the mood to enforce legislation enacted in the 1920s as part of the outlawing of liquor sales during Prohibition. Apparently alcohol was more dangerous when imbibed interracially. The appeal of ghetto glitz reached its apex at Harlem's Savoy Ballroom, where integrated crowds of up to 4,000 danced to music provided by the most famous dance bands of the era.

Few of Harlem's residents, however, could afford the Savoy. The world of cabarets, concerts, and publication contracts that swirled around the notables of the Harlem Renaissance meant little to the majority of women who toiled daily as domestic workers, or to men carrying home a few dollars each day for pushing a broom or tending a machine. They caught their music at rent parties, all-night affairs in tightly packed apartments where a quarter at the door purchased food, drink, and live entertainment, with the proceeds used to pay the rent. Or they got music through a new phenomenon known as "race" records.

By mid-decade the strong economy had brought enough secure employment in most cities to permit many black families in cities across the country to purchase phonographs. After Okeh Records took the plunge

Okeh Records was the first label to record Duke Ellington and his orchestra. But this tune, from the revue "Blackbirds of 1928," was written by two white songwriters, Dorothy Fields and Jimmy McHugh.

in 1920 and issued Mamie Smith's *Crazy Blues* (which sold thousands of copies), other recording companies jumped into the market. Race records brought substantial profits to white record company owners. Black Swan Records, whose advertisements truthfully trumpeted "The Only Genuine Colored Record," enjoyed only brief success, in part because of its commitment to maintaining a catalogue of more respectable (but not profitable) classical music in addition to blues recordings. The race-records market remained nearly exclusively African American, reaching even into small coal mining towns in West Virginia, where one resident later recalled the importance of the discs during the 1920s:

Every payday we'd bottle up the home brew we'd been getting ready and mama would send us kids down to the store to get the latest blues records. Everybody else we knew would be there too and we'd carry those records home, stacked in our arms. All the Negroes lived together in that "company" town and you could go from street to street and hear those blues records blasting out from the open doors.

Sustaining an African-American voice in film proved more difficult. The first attempt came in 1915 with the establishment of the Lincoln Motion Picture Company. Noble Johnson, an actor with experience at Universal Studios, made the films in Los Angeles. His brother George took care of the marketing after finishing his shift at the Omaha, Nebraska, post office. They drew support from both communities, especially in Los Angeles, with its pair of African-American hotels, a black baseball league, an "African cafe," and an active NAACP branch.

Drawing on the emerging Watts ghetto for his screenplays, Noble Johnson sought "to picture the Negro as he is in his every day life, a human being with human inclination, and one of talent and intellect." George Johnson developed strong relationships with black newspapers, and Lincoln films were able to take advantage of the wartime migration to cities to build an audience.

The story of the Johnson brothers, however, also reveals the difficulties of black enterprise and the obstacles faced by African Americans committed to using the new tools of mass culture (at that time, radio, newspapers, and motion pictures) to provide honest depictions of black life. Lack of money and restricted access to distribution networks and credit undermined the company's ability to compete with white-owned film companies.

Nor did the Johnsons reach beyond a black audience; whites showed no interest in their films. The Lincoln Motion Picture Company folded in 1921. Another independent black filmmaker, Oscar Micheaux, would continue working through the 1920s and 1930s, but on the whole the film industry would be dominated by large studios turning out films with either no black characters or African Americans appearing in stereotypical and demeaning comical roles.

Surveying the state of black America in 1925, one young African-American scholar concluded that the business of producing culture was less indicative of the power and potential of the New Negro than the culture of the black businessman. E. Franklin Frazier, at the beginning of a long

The movie Black Gold, *released in 1928, was the inspirational story of oilfield workers in the all-black city of Tatums, Oklahoma. Nearby Langston, named for a great-uncle of poet Langston Hughes, was the first of several all-black towns settled in the former Indian Territory.*

THE STORY OF BLACK GOLD

Since Oil had been discovered on the Oklahoma Range, around the little town of Tatums, ranching had been abandoned. Mart Ashton, owner of the Bar Circle Ranch, was the newest victim of the Black Gold Fever. The oil drill was boring a hole to wealth or poverty, into which he had sunk all his cash and even sacrificed his fine herd of cattle to raise cash to sink the first well on his ranch. On an adjoining claim, the Ohio Company brings in a well and this forces Ashton to drill an offset well within 30 days or lose the permit to drill on his own ranch. Pete Barkley, Ashton's oil driller, refuses to drill farther until he is paid $4,000, due him. Barkley is scheming with Walter Worder, Cashier of the Ranchman's National Bank to secure Ashton's permit by delaying work on his well. Ashton manages to borrow the money to force Barkley to continue drilling, but Worder and Barkley snare him in a plot and accuse him of robbing the Bank. Ace Brand, Ashton's Foreman, knows he is innocent, but is unable to prove it. Alice Anderson, daughter of the President of the Ranchman's National, and in love with Ace, does everything in her power, to prove Ashton's innocence, but to no avail. With Ashton in jail, his well idle, and only 7 days left to bring it in, it is up to Ace, Alice and Peg Reynolds the one lonely hand on the Bar Circle to bring in the well securely.

As to how they do this, through superhuman effort, and without sleep for 48 hours, fighting a band of crooks—only to discover it is a dry hole—with apparently everything lost—and Ashton in jail—makes an absorbing story of action and thrills—with a great surprise at the end, and when everything is cleared up. Does Mart Ashton discover BLACK GOLD on his Ranch?

Norman Studios Presents

Black Gold

ALL COLORED CAST

Action!

Thrills!

·A SUPER·FEATURE·

career as a distinguished sociologist, stated his minority opinion in one of the essays of Alain Locke's anthology, *The New Negro*.

He urged his readers to look beyond Harlem toward Durham, North Carolina, where African Americans owned thriving insurance companies and banks. "Durham offers none of the color and creative life we find among Negroes in New York City. . . . It is not a place where men write and dream, but a place where men calculate and work." His essay pointed to black economic dynamism, not cultural achievement, as the truly important change in the 1920s. Black financiers and businessmen along with a growing industrial working class would eventually merge black America with white America. When this happened race would cease to be important; what would matter was class.

A small group of young activists argued that class already was the division that mattered. The challenge was to convince black Americans that as workers their interests were best represented not by the middle-class NAACP and National Urban League, but by the labor and socialist movements, which claimed to speak for all workers. At the same time white workers would have to be convinced that black workers were allies, rather than rivals.

Calling itself the voice of the "New Crowd Negro," a new magazine called *The Messenger* was launched in 1917 by A. Philip Randolph and Chandler Owen. Both men were college educated and had migrated from the South to Harlem. Their notion of a "New Negro" had less to do with culture than with politics—in particular socialist politics. Randolph and Owen opposed American involvement in World War I. Dismissing the war as a battle among European imperialists, they tied the oppression of African Americans to colonialism in Africa (the political and ecomonic control of most of Africa by European nations) and to the oppression of the working class around the world.

Both union activity and socialist politics were becoming increasingly visible in African-American communities in the early part of the 20th century. The leading black socialist of that time was probably George Washington Woodbey. Born a slave in Tennessee in 1854, Woodbey educated himself after the Civil War, despite less than two years of formal schooling. He moved to San Diego in 1903 (like so many other migrants, part of a family chain—he first went there to visit his mother), where he served as a minister and as a socialist orator and pamphleteer.

Woodbey's visibility in the movement in some ways highlights socialism's weakness among African Americans. He stood out among socialists for the attention he gave in his speeches to the relationship between racial oppression and class conflict, a link that many socialists either ignored or treated superficially. Although generally less committed to white supremacy than most other white Americans, the socialists seldom directly challenged prevailing notions about race. Moreover, Woodbey's status as a minister is important. Most African Americans were likely to look within, rather than outside the black community for leadership—to their preachers, editors, business owners, lawyers, and educators.

By the end of the 1910s radical politics was developing deeper roots in some black communities, most notably Harlem. Hubert Harrison, a leading street-corner orator and Socialist party activist before World War I, broke with the party in 1917. He proclaimed the need for a combination of black nationalism and socialism, with "race first" as the cornerstone.

Harrison frequently crossed paths with Cyril Briggs, founder in 1917 of the African Blood Brotherhood. Briggs described his organization as "a revolutionary secret order" dedicated to armed resistance to lynching, opposition to all forms of racial discrimination, and voting rights for black Southerners. He also sought the unionization of black workers and African-

American control of political institutions in parts of the United States where they were a majority of the population.

The brotherhood also opposed American participation in World War I and linked the struggle for black liberation in the United States to the battle against European colonization in Africa. The organization never grew beyond a few thousand, but by the early 1920s had expanded from its Harlem base to places as diverse as the West Indies and West Virginia. Like Hubert Harrison and George Washington Woodbey, the African Blood Brotherhood is significant because of its place in the broad range of African-American thought in the early 20th century. It also is an example of the participation of black Americans in international debates about colonialism, politics, and race.

Organizing in Harlem for the nearly successful Socialist candidate for mayor in 1917, Randolph and Owen managed to attract thousands of black voters to the socialist banner. But success was short-lived and localized. In general the Socialist party failed to attract black voters, in part because it was unwilling to take a strong stand against Jim Crow.

The Communist party attracted few African Americans during the 1920s. These were mainly intellectuals impressed with its forthright stands against colonialism in Africa and racism in the United States. The party would win many black supporters for the help it lent to African Americans in civil rights and economic issues during the Great Depression of the 1930s. But in the 1920s attempts by the Communist party to organize black workers were so unsuccessful that A. Philip Randolph dismissed black Communists as a group that could meet in a phone booth.

Not that Randolph, Owen, or other African-American labor organizers had done much better. Several attempts had been made to organize unions with mainly black membership. All had failed, mostly because of resistance from white unions. By 1925, the *Messenger* was barely surviving after dropping from its peak circulation of 26,000 in 1919. Chandler Owen left to work for another publication in Chicago, and Randolph began to rethink his attitudes towards the American Federation of Labor (AFL).

The only route to black unionization seemed to be inclusion in existing labor organizations. The NAACP and the National Urban League had tried this route in 1918–19, urging black workers to join unions wherever they were accepted on an equal basis. But few unions would take blacks on an equal basis with their white members. In his earlier years as a radical Randolph had viewed the AFL as not only racist, but also too willing to accept the class structures created by capitalism. Now he decided that the AFL's approach to unionism—accepting the system and trying to secure workers a larger share of corporate profits—was the best way for black workers to move toward the standard of living that unionized white workers had attained.

Randolph began organizing an all-black union whose agenda resembled that of mainstream white craft unions: higher wages, job security, and collective bargaining. The Brotherhood of Sleeping Car Porters and Maids struggled against the Pullman company for a decade, winning partial victories in 1926 and 1929 and complete recognition in 1937. Despite considerable opposition and only after tireless insistence on Randolph's part, the Brotherhood also became the first African-American union awarded a full charter by the American Federation of Labor. Its organizing battles and its grass-roots leadership would eventually provide the basis for a half-century of civil rights struggles in cities across the United States.

For most black Americans in the 1920s, however, unionization did not represent an option. The Harlem Renaissance was a distant phenomenon, not very important even to many Harlemites. What captured the imagination of the black masses was another movement rooted in Harlem, the Universal Negro Improvement Association (UNIA). The organization was inseparable from its founder, chief spokes-man, and strategist, Marcus M. Garvey.

Garvey founded the UNIA in 1914 on his native West Indian island of Jamaica, at the time still a British colony. He attracted little support for his organization and brought his vision of a liberated Africa and a fully emancipated black population to the United States two years later. That vision and Garvey's expression of it drew heavily on the rhetoric surrounding World War I, which had been justified by the United States and its allies as a fight for "self-determination." Garvey compared his cause to that of the Irish revolutionaries fighting for independence and the Zionists struggling for a Jewish state in Palestine. His version called for the self-determination of Africans across the globe—"Africa for the Africans."

Garvey began with the assumption that the United States, like the British in Jamaica, was hopelessly committed to white supremacy. Racial equality was impossible, integra-

The charismatic Marcus Garvey promoted racial pride and economic self-sufficiency for blacks. "Up you mighty race," he proclaimed, "you can accomplish what you will."

tion and assimilation absurd. Unlike Alain Locke, James Weldon Johnson, Jessie Fauset, and other driving forces behind the Harlem Renaissance who saw the flowering of African-American culture as a step toward equality and even integration, and unlike E. Franklin Frazier's vision of a black business class providing the basis for assimilation, Garvey saw culture and business as the foundation of a separate black world. Like Booker T. Washington, he told black Americans that they had to reshape their perspective, casting off all traces of dependence on whites.

Garvey did not, however, share Washington's vision of the two races working side by side in cooperation, with blacks eventually winning respect through proper behavior and modest prosperity. Whites would never willingly permit blacks to rise, warned Garvey; they respected only naked power. "A race without authority and power is a race without respect," declared Garvey. Criticizing the NAACP's strategy of seeking justice through lawsuits and legislation, he observed that "there is not justice, but strength." Blacks, therefore, had to compete. They had to establish independent nations in Africa, independent businesses in the United States, and a framework of black institutions independent of white influence.

The UNIA would provide that framework. Its newspaper, the *Negro World,* attained a circulation of 50,000–60,000 in the mid-1920s. Among African-American newspapers, only the *Chicago Defender* reached a wider audience. The UNIA established businesses, especially laundries and groceries, retail operations that could rely on a black clientele and employ

A UNIA parade in 1924, photographed by the noted black photographer James Van Der Zee.

143

UNIA members. Most visibly, Garvey founded the Black Star Line Steamship Company, funded by sales of stock to UNIA members. To buy shares was to invest in the race. Garvey promised profits, employment for black seamen, and transportation for African-American passengers traveling to Africa to lead that continent's struggle against European colonial domination.

These enterprises were funded and publicized at mass meetings, amid elaborate pageantry designed to foster racial pride in addition to organizational enthusiasm. Weekly meetings were held in UNIA Liberty Halls across the United States. Frequent parades featured uniformed Black Cross Nurses, African Legions, and other divisions, each with its own officers and insignia. Marching under banners proclaiming "We Want a Black Civilization" and "God and the Negro Shall Triumph," Garvey's followers militantly repudiated white supremacy.

The message—that black people in the 1920s could accomplish anything if they put their mind to it and did not stop to worry about white folks—closely resembled the sensibilities underlying the Great Migration. That message resonated powerfully. One man who had grown up in Cleveland later recalled "standing on Central Avenue, watching a parade one Sunday afternoon when thousands of Garvey legionnaires, resplendent in their uniforms, marched by. When Garvey rode by in his plumed hat, I got an emotional lift, which swept me above the poverty and the prejudice by which my life was limited."

At its height between 1923 and 1926 the UNIA counted more than 700 branches in 38 states, in addition to a substantial body of support in the Caribbean and Central America. Some of these branches probably consisted of a handful of enthusiasts, or perhaps even a single household. Others, in large cities, numbered in the thousands. Perhaps most striking is the geographic diversity, ranging across country and city and from the Northeast to the Midwest, South, and Pacific coast. The organization claimed 6 million members, but 500,000 is probably a more realistic estimate. At least another half-million supporters never paid dues but counted themselves among Garvey's followers. The UNIA was easily the largest African-American mass movement the United States had ever seen.

The moment, however, was brief. The Black Star Line was a financial disaster, due in part to bad luck associated with calamitous weather on its initial freight run and in part to weak management. The company's bankruptcy provided ammunition to Garvey's enemies, a list that included

The Black Star Line, established by Marcus Garvey in 1919, was supposed to provide black Americans with jobs, transportation, and profits, but it failed after only four years of operation.

nearly all of the established African-American leadership. To radicals like A. Philip Randolph and Cyril Briggs, Garvey had too much faith in capitalism. To the moderates in the NAACP he was too inflammatory. Respectable middle-class community leaders found his parades embarrassing. To advise black Americans to look to Africa for salvation (actually a minor part of the Garvey agenda, but one that has remained most visible in the public mind), was foolish, they argued. It played into the hands of white racists who declared that blacks could never become true Americans.

Editor Robert Abbott of the *Chicago Defender,* an unyielding opponent of racism but a firm believer in American institutions, hated Garvey so much that he banished mention of the UNIA from his newspaper. His readers learned absolutely nothing about the active Chicago chapter, even though it had 9,000 members. In 1922 Garvey confirmed his opponents' worst fears. He attended a meeting of the Ku Klux Klan and declared that the Klan was more honest about race in the United States than the NAACP and other black organizations. At Abbott's urging Garvey was indicted for fraud in 1923 in connection with the sale of shares in the Black Star Line. Most likely he was less guilty of fraud than of incompetence. Nevertheless, he was convicted and jailed until his deportation from the United States in 1927.

Garvey remained a hero to thousands of black Americans, especially small businesspeople and working-class men and women. Years later Malcolm X would recall accompanying his father to UNIA meetings during the 1930s, long after the movement's decline. In his autobiography, he recalled the dozen or so people packed into a living room and was struck by

> how differently they all acted, although they were the same people who jumped and shouted in church. But in these meetings both they and my father were more intense, more intelligent and down to earth. It made me feel the same way. . . . I remember how the meetings always closed with my father saying, several times, and the people chanting after him, "Up, you mighty race, you can accomplish what you will."

EPILOGUE

The spring of 1927 is remembered along the southern stretches of the Mississippi River as the season the rains came. By June, despite continuing efforts to reinforce the earthworks, the levees erected to protect riverside communities from flooding had been breached. The thick yellow water moved across the countryside, displacing approximately a million people in Arkansas, Louisiana, and Mississippi. Thousands of these were sharecroppers, most of them African American, who planted, cultivated, and picked cotton on the plantations of the fertile Mississippi Delta.

The flood itself knew no racial bounds; black and white families were forced from their homes. But here equality ended. Relief efforts were spearheaded by the Red Cross, which established relief stations and refugee camps—separated, of course, by race, according to Jim Crow laws. In nearly all cases (Baton Rouge was a notable exception) whites sat at tables for their meals; blacks stood or sat on the ground. Planters believed that the camps should be kept as spartan as possible, so that their wage workers and tenants would not get too accustomed to such comforts as complete meals, health care, and recreational facilities.

Even more important, while camps for Mexicans and whites had unrestricted access, National Guardsmen regulated movement in and out of the camps for African Americans. White officials wanted black workers on call for the backbreaking work of trying to shore up the levees. They also wanted to assure that black Southerners would return to their landlords after the crisis. In essence this meant virtual incarceration of black refugees in what black leaders later referred to as "concentration camps" and "peonage pens." It also meant keeping watch against outsiders trying to recruit workers either for plantations elsewhere in the South or for Northern industry. As the commander of the Mississippi National Guard explained, his mission required him to establish conditions that would enable each planter after the crisis to claim "his niggers," but not "any other but *his own niggers.*"

This belief by whites that they owned African-American labor had a long tradition in the South. During the Great Migration, some white Southerners had readily wished the northbound migrants good riddance. But landlords and others dependent on black labor took strong measures to keep their workers in place. Recruiters were arrested. The *Defender* was confiscated from the mails. Some railroad stations were closed down, while at others police drove prospective black passengers from the platforms. The Southern labor system still depended upon the restriction of African Americans to jobs within their local labor market. Little had changed by 1927, when the great flood uprooted thousands of black families who until then had withstood the pressures of declining cotton prices throughout the 1920s and continued to stake their future on the land.

Those who had left during the Great Migration encountered a different kind of immobility—at least beyond a certain point. Their footholds in Northern industry seemed secure in the 1920s, and many workers had even climbed a rung from unskilled to semiskilled jobs. But as the decade came to an end, it became increasingly clear that few would rise any further. With employers generally unwilling to promote African Americans to supervisory positions, blacks found themselves stuck on the lower rungs of the industrial job ladder.

Moreover, despite the growth of an African-American clientele, retail stores in black neighborhoods tended to follow the pattern of Harlem's 24 A&P grocery stores, which confined their black work force to a total of nine errand boys. "Don't buy where you can't work" campaigns had only minimal effect, producing a handful of jobs mainly for light-skinned women. Black-owned businesses provided few alternatives. Most were small operations, employing only the proprietor and perhaps a family member.

To make matters even worse, the end of the 1920s brought a new crisis, the Great Depression. The Great Depression is generally associated with the crash of the stock market in 1929, but for many working-class Americans the initial impact had already struck before this event in the form of decreased production and job insecurity.

Last hired and first fired, African-Americans workers were already facing hardships by 1929. But with the crash came cascading waves of factory shut-downs, and mass unemployment in every sector of the economy. In the South farmers accustomed to scratching a bare living out of the soil now struggled to avoid starvation. In the cities, unemployment skyrocketed, to approximate-ly 15 percent of the work force by 1930, with the rate among African Americans probably in the range of 30 percent. These rates would increase even further during the next two years.

Even domestic workers, who often could find positions when their hus-bands and sons could not, spent more time looking for work and less time on the job. Nor could people rely on their savings, with banks across the country closing their doors during the early years of the crisis. Banks in black commu-nities failed at a rate even higher than those in other neighborhoods.

As the 1930s opened, therefore, thousands of African Americans looked at the future and the past much like Bernice Avery, a black South-erner who had moved to Detroit with her parents in 1919. Her family had moved into a neighborhood of shacks, but shacks that the residents owned on land that they also owned. In 1919 they had bigger plans for that land: "We all knew that these were our temporary homes—someday we would build a beautiful permanent home with running water instead of the old pump, and modern sanitation to take the place of the outside toilets and the tin tub to bathe in."

By the 1930s, the outside toilets and tin tubs remained; these homes were among the most unsanitary and rundown in the city. The community's physical deterioration meant that life was hard. The tragic inability of resi-dents to move toward fulfilling their dreams produced a different kind of pain.

In many cases this disappointment extended to the hopes for the next generation. In cities north and south, many black teenagers learned that a high school diploma opened doors marked "whites only." Although black chil-dren in Northern cities were less likely to drop out of school at the beginning of the decade than their immigrant counterparts, increasing numbers would pose the same question that a Chicago juvenile probation officer frequently heard from black truants: "What work can I get if I go through school?"

The answer was hardly encouraging. In one all-black girls' high school in Pittsburgh, for example, students told interviewers of their ambitions to white collar employment; after graduation, however, more than half could find no

Graduates of I.C. Norcom High School, Portsmouth, Virginia, 1920.

employment other than cleaning homes and cooking meals. Given the curriculum in some places, this was hardly surprising. As the student body of a school changed from white to black in the 1920s, teachers' and administrators' expectations about the students often changed as well. By 1933, less than half of the tenth-grade students at Cleveland's Central High took any mathematics classes; the home economics classes were likely to teach laundering skills. Both academic and vocational courses that students at other schools took for granted no longer were taught at Central, where black children were denied the opportunity to study German, Spanish, stenography, or bookkeeping.

In 1940 a United States Office of Education study came to the obvious conclusion about the relationship between education and work during the previous decade: "The more schooling a black person achieved the more dissatisfied he was with his job."

By the time of the Great Depression, there already were many who had become too cynical, too pessimistic to dream. Clifford Burke, a teamster in a lumberyard, summed up this feeling. "The Negro," Burke recalled, "was born in depression. It didn't mean too much to him, the Great American Depression, as you call it. There was no such thing. The best he could be was a janitor or a porter or shoeshine boy. It only became official when it hit the white man."

CHRONOLOGY

1894

U.S. Department of Agriculture agent at Corpus Christi, Texas, submits first report of a weevil that destroys cotton bolls

1895

Publication of *A Red Record* by Ida B. Wells

1896

In *Plessy* v. *Ferguson*, U.S. Supreme Court establishes principle that racial segregation is constitutional as long as "separate but equal" facilities are provided

1896

Founding of the National Association of Colored Women

1900

Founding of the Women's Convention of the National Baptist Convention

1900

Founding of National Negro Business League

1901

Publication of *Up from Slavery* by Booker T. Washington

1901

Boston Guardian established by William Monroe Trotter

1901

President William McKinley assassinated; Vice President Theodore Roosevelt becomes President

1903

Publication of *The Souls of Black Folk* by W. E. B. Du Bois

1905

Chicago Defender established by Robert S. Abbott

JULY 1905

Niagara Movement founded

AUGUST 1906

Incident at army base in Brownsville, Texas, results in dismissal without honor of three companies of the 25th Infantry, an all-black unit

SEPTEMBER 1906

Race riot in Atlanta

1908

William Howard Taft elected President

1910

Founding of the National Association for the Advancement of Colored People

1912

Woodrow Wilson elected President of the United States

1914

World War I begins

1914

Founding of the Universal Negro Improvement Association in Jamaica

1915

U.S. Supreme Court declares Grandfather Clause unconstitutional in *Guinn* v. *United States*

NOVEMBER 1915

Booker T. Washington dies

1916

Great Migration begins

1916

Marcus Garvey arrives in the U.S.

APRIL 1917

U.S. enters World War I

NOVEMBER 1918

World War I ends

1919

Race riots break out in 26 cities across the U.S.

1920

20th Amendment to the Constitution ratified, providing women the right to vote. Black women in the South, like black men, remain largely disfranchised

1920

Founding of National Negro [Baseball] League

1921-22

Shuffle Along, a musical written, produced by, and starring African Americans, is the most popular show on Broadway

1923

Marcus Garvey imprisoned for mail fraud

1925

Founding of the Brotherhood of Sleeping Car Porters

1925

Publication of *The New Negro*, edited by Alain Locke

1928

Oscar DePriest (Republican, Chicago) becomes the first African American elected to Congress from a district north of the Mason-Dixon line

1929

Stock market crashes marking the beginning of the Great Depression

FURTHER READING

GENERAL AFRICAN-AMERICAN HISTORY

Bennett, Lerone, Jr. *Before the Mayflower: A History of Black America.* 6th rev. ed. New York: Viking Penguin, 1988.

———. *The Shaping of Black America.* New York: Viking Penguin, 1993.

Foner, Philip S. *History of Black Americans: From Africa to the Emergence of the Cotton Kingdom.* Westport, Conn.: Greenwood, 1975.

Franklin, John H., and Alfred A. Moss, Jr. *From Slavery to Freedom: A History of Negro Americans.* 6th ed. New York: Knopf, 1987.

Franklin, John Hope, and August Meier. *Black Leaders of the 20th Century.* Urbana: University of Illinois Press, 1982.

Gates, Henry L., Jr. *A Chronology of African-American History from 1445–1980.* New York: Amistad, 1980.

Giddings, Paula. *When and Where I Enter: The Impact of Black Women on Race and Sex in America.* New York: Bantam, 1985.

Harding, Vincent. *There Is a River: The Black Struggle for Freedom in America.* San Diego: Harcourt Brace, 1981.

Hine, Darlene C., et al., eds. *Black Women in America.* Brooklyn, N.Y.: Carlson, 1993.

Jones, Jacqueline. *Labor of Love, Labor of Sorrow: Black Women, Work, and the Family from Slavery to the Present.* New York: Basic Books, 1985.

Meltzer, Milton. *The Black Americans: A History in Their Own Words.* Rev. ed. New York: HarperCollins, 1984.

Mintz, Sidney W., and Richard Price. *The Birth of African-American Culture: An Anthropological Perspective.* Boston: Beacon Press, 1992.

Quarles, Benjamin. *The Negro in the Making of America.* 3rd ed. New York: Macmillan, 1987.

Salzman, Jack, David Lionel Smith, and Cornel West, eds. *Encyclopedia of African-American Culture and History.* 5 vols. New York: Simon & Schuster Macmillan, 1996.

LEADERSHIP AND INSTITUTIONAL DEVELOPMENT

Anderson, James. *The Education of Blacks in the South, 1880–1935.* Chapel Hill: University of North Carolina Press, 1988.

Brown, Elsa Barkley. "Womanist Consciousness: Maggie Lena Walker and the Independent Order of Saint Luke," *Signs,* vol. 14, no. 3 (1989): 610–633.

Du Bois, William Edward Burkhardt. *The Souls of Black Folk.* 1903. Reprint, New York: Vintage, 1990.

Garvey, Amy Jacques. *The Philosophy and Opinions of Marcus Garvey,* with an Introduction by Robert A. Hill. New York: 1992.

Harlan, Lewis R. *Booker T. Washington: The Wizard of Tuskegee, 1901–1915.* New York: Oxford University Press, 1983.

Higginbotham, Evelyn Brooks. *Righteous Discontent: The Women's Movement in the Black Baptist Church, 1880–1920.* Cambridge: Harvard University Press, 1993.

Ottley, Roi. *The Lonely Warrior: The Life and Times of Robert S. Abbott.* Chicago: Henry Regnery & Co., 1955.

Salem, Dorothy. *To Better Our World: Black Women in Organized Reform, 1890–1920,* volume 14 in *Black Women in United States History,* Darlene Clark Hine, ed. Brooklyn, N.Y.: Carlson, 1990.

Shaw, Stephanie. *What a Woman Ought to Be and to Do: Black Professional Women Workers during the Jim Crow Era*. Chicago: University of Chicago Press, 1996.

BIOGRAPHIES AND AUTOBIOGRAPHIES

Adair, Gene. *George Washington Carver*. New York: Chelsea House, 1989.

Haynes, Richard M. *Ida B. Wells: Antilynching Crusader*. Austin, Tex.: Raintree Steck-Vaughn, 1994.

Johnson, James Weldon. *Along This Way: The Autobiography of James Weldon Johnson*. New York: Viking Press, 1933.

Johnson, Lyman T. *The Rest of the Dream: The Black Odyssey of Lyman Johnson*. Edited by Wade Hall. Lexington, Ky.: University of Kentucky Press, 1988.

Pickens, William. *Bursting Bonds: The Heir of Slaves*. Boston: Jordan & More Press, 1923.

Rosengarten, Theodore. *All God's Dangers: The Life of Nate Shaw*. New York: Knopf, 1975.

Schroeder, Alan. *Booker T. Washington*. New York: Chelsea House, 1992.

Tarry, Ellen. *The Third Door: The Autobiography of an American Negro Woman*. New York: Guild Press, 1966 (expanded ed.; orig. publication, 1955).

Washington, Booker T. *Up from Slavery*. 1901. Reprint, New York: Penguin, 1986.

Wright, Richard. *Black Boy: A Record of Childhood and Youth*. New York: Harper & Row, 1937.

AFRICAN-AMERICAN CULTURE

Cripps, Thomas. *Slow Fade to Black: The Negro in American Film, 1900–1942*. New York: Oxford University Press, 1977.

Huggins, Nathan I. *Harlem Renaissance*. New York: Oxford University Press, 1971.

———. *Voices from the Harlem Renaissance*. New York: Oxford University Press, 1976.

Johnson-Feelings, Dianne, ed. *The Best of The Brownies' Book*. New York: Oxford University Press, 1996.

Levine, Lawrence L. *Black Culture and Black Consciousness: Afro-American Folk Thought from Slavery to Freedom*. New York: Oxford University Press, 1977.

Lewis, David Levering. *When Harlem Was in Vogue*. New York: Knopf, 1981.

Locke, Alain. *The New Negro: An Interpretation*. 1925. Reprint, New York: Arno, 1968.

The Studio Museum in Harlem. *Harlem Renaissance: Art of Black America*. New York: Harry N. Abrams, 1987.

Watson, Steven. *The Harlem Renaissance: Hub of African-American Culture, 1920–1930*. New York: Pantheon Books, 1995.

COMMUNITY STUDIES

Daniels, Douglas Henry. *Black Pioneers: A Social and Cultural History of Black San Francisco*. Philadelphia: Temple University Press, 1980.

Du Bois, William Edward Burkhardt. *The Philadelphia Negro: A Social Study*. 1899. Reprint, New York: Benjamin Blom, 1967.

Kusmer, Kenneth L. *A Ghetto Takes Shape: Black Cleveland, 1870–1930*. Urbana: University of Illinois Press, 1976.

Lewis, Earl. *In Their Own Interests: Race, Class, and Power in Twentieth-Century Norfolk, Virginia*. Berkeley: University of California Press, 1991.

Spear, Allan H. *Black Chicago: The Making of a Negro Ghetto, 1890–1920.* Chicago: University of Chicago Press, 1967.

Taylor, Quintard. *The Forging of a Black Community: Seattle's Central District from 1870 through the Civil Rights Era.* Seattle: University of Washington Press, 1994.

Trotter, Joe William. *Black Milwaukee: The Making of the Industrial Proletariat, 1915–1945.* Urbana: University of Illinois Press, 1985.

Wright, George. *Life Behind a Veil: Blacks in Louisville, Kentucky, 1865–1930.* Baton Rouge: Louisiana State University Press, 1985.

THE GREAT MIGRATION AND WORLD WAR I

Adero, Malaika ed., *Up South: Stories, Studies, and Letters of the Century's Black Migrations.* New York: New Press, 1993.

Crew, Spencer R. *Field to Factory: Afro-American Migration 1915–1940.* Washington, D.C.: National Museum of American History, Smithsonian Institution, 1987.

Gottlieb, Peter. *Making Their Own Way: Southern Blacks' Migration to Pittsburgh, 1916-1930.* Urbana: University of Illinois Press, 1987.

Grossman, James R. *Land of Hope: Chicago, Black Southerners, and the Great Migration.* Chicago: University of Chicago Press, 1989.

Henri, Florette, and Arthur Barbeau. *The Unknown Soldiers: Black American Troops in World War I.* Philadelphia: Temple University Press, 1974.

Trotter, Joe W., ed. *The Great Migration in Historical Perspective: New Dimensions of Race, Class and Gender.* Bloomington: Indiana University Press, 1991.

RACE RELATIONS

Ayers, Edward L. *The Promise of the New South: Life After Reconstruction.* New York: Oxford University Press, 1993.

Dittmer, John. *Black Georgia in the Progressive Era, 1900-1920.* Urbana: University of Illinois Press, 1977.

Hair, William Ivy. *Carnival of Fury: Robert Charles and the New Orleans Race Riot of 1900.* Baton Rouge: Louisiana State University Press, 1976.

McMillen, Neil. *Dark Journey: Black Mississippians in the Age of Jim Crow.* Urbana: University of Illinois Press, 1989.

Tuttle, William M., Jr. *Race Riot: Chicago in the Red Summer of 1919.* New York: Atheneum, 1970.

Williamson, Joel. *A Rage for Order: Black/White Relations in the American South since Emancipation.* New York: Oxford University Press, 1986.

WORK AND THE ECONOMY

Clark-Lewis, Elizabeth. *Living In, Living Out: African American Domestics in Washington, D.C., 1910–1940.* Washington, D.C.: Smithsonian Institution Press, 1994.

Harris, William H. *The Harder We Run: Black Workers since the Civil War.* New York: Oxford University Press, 1982.

Jones, Jacqueline. *The Dispossessed: America's Underclass from the Civil War to the Present.* New York: Basic Books, 1992.

Trotter, Joe William. *Coal, Class, and Color: Blacks in Southern West Virginia, 1915–32.* Urbana: University of Illinois Press, 1990.

Wright, Gavin. *Old South, New South: Revolutions in the Southern Economy since the Civil War.* New York: Basic Books, 1986.

INDEX

ACKNOWLEDGMENTS

Writing for young adults carries little prestige in academic culture. Conversely, publishers of such books often dismiss scholars as either unwilling or unable to present their ideas to this audience. I am grateful to my colleagues at the Newberry Library, especially Richard Brown and Fred Hoxie, for their encouragement. And I am grateful to Oxford University Press for undertaking this project, which I hope will be as rewarding to young readers as it has been to me. Most of all, however, I wish to thank my colleagues Earl Lewis and Robin Kelley for inviting to participate in this series. They have provided superb editorial service as well, offering useful suggestions at the outset and thoughtfully criticizing a draft of the manuscript. Nancy Toff at Oxford University Press has contributed a wonderful combination of patience and prodding, not only with deadlines but also with prose.

Writing without footnotes is liberating. But it also makes it difficult to acknowledge one's intellectual debts beyond the citations in a bibliography. Leon Litwack, Laura Edwards, Earl Lewis, Kathy Conzen, and Elsa Barkley Brown will find their intellectual fingerprints in various parts of the book; I thank them for their conversation, collegiality, and insight. I have never met Charles Hardy, but he immediately will recognize that I could never have written the prologue without his work.

Without Ann Billingsley I might never have written this at all. Her support, encouragement, patience (and timely impatience), and good sense have made it easier to complete this book and all the other projects that interfered with the smooth progress I once naively envisioned. Ruth and Alice have learned how difficult it is to write even a relatively small book but how rewarding as well; I hope they haven't learned that one can, in fact, miss a deadline.

Picture Credits

Atlanta History Center: 93, 104; Carnegie Hall Archives: 88; Chicago Historical Society: 105, 128, 129; Cincinnati Historical Society: 37 (neg. 116-136C-4030), 67 (neg. B-96-203), 115 (neg. B-96-204), 116 (lung association, neg. C-6); Florida State Archives: 12, 14, 27, 30, 38, 51, 54, 57, 66, 80, 83, 139; George Meany Memorial Archives: 122 (neg. 664); Hampton University Museum, Hampton, Virginia. Charles White, detail from *The Contribution of the Negro to Democracy in America,* 1943: 9; Illinois Labor History Society: 121; James Van Der Zee, courtesy Donna Van Der Zee: 7, 20, 143; courtesy John Carter Brown Library at Brown University: 71; Kansas State Historical Society, Topeka, Kansas: 41; Library of Congress: 15, 24, 52, 56, 65, 68-69, 77, 91, 94, 95, 96, 98, 101, 107, 108, 135, 136, 142, 149; Maggie L. Walker National Historic Site, Richmond, Virginia: 64; Mississippi Department of Archives and History: 58, 61; Missouri Historical Society, St. Louis: 118; National Archives: cover, 10, 22, 29, 35, 45, 47, 87, 130, 132, 133; Negro Leagues Baseball Museum, Inc.: 79; Oklahoma Historical Society, Archives and Manuscript Division: 100; Schomburg Center for Research in Black Culture, New York Public Library, Astor, Lenox, and Tilden Foundations: 2, 42, 137, 145; State Historical Society of Wisconsin: 84 (neg. WHi (x3) 37869); Temple University Libraries, Urban Archives: 17; Texas State Library, Archives Division: 32; University of Illinois at Chicago, University Library, Department of Special Collections: 62 (Lloyd O. Lewis Family Papers), 113 (Arthur and Graham Aldis Papers), 114 (Chicago Urban League Papers); University of Pittsburgh, Archives of Industrial Society, Urban League of Pittsburgh Collection: 74, 90, 110, 124, 126; Western Reserve Historical Society, Cleveland, Ohio: 73, 76.

JAMES R. GROSSMAN ◇◇◇

James R. Grossman is the director of the Dr. William M. Scholl Center for Family and Community History at the Newberry Library. Dr. Grossman has taught at the University of Chicago and at the University of California, San Diego. He is the author of *Land of Hope: Chicago, Black Southerners, and the Great Migration* and the editor of *The Frontier in American Culture.*

ROBIN D. G. KELLEY ◇◇◇

Robin D. G. Kelley is professor of history and Africana studies at New York University. He previously taught history and African-American studies at the University of Michigan. He is the author of *Hammer and Hoe: Alabama Communists during the Great Depression,* which received the Eliot Rudwick Prize of the Organization of American Historians and was named Outstanding Book on Human Rights by the Gustavus Myers Center for the Study of Human Rights in the United States. Professor Kelley is also the author of *Race Rebels: Culture, Politics, and the Black Working Class* and co-editor of *Imagining Home: Class, Culture, and Nationalism in the African Diaspora.*

EARL LEWIS ◇◇◇

Earl Lewis is professor of history and Afroamerican studies at the University of Michigan. He served as director of the university's Center for Afroamerican and African Studies from 1990 to 1993. Professor Lewis is the author of *In Their Own Interests: Race, Class and Power in Twentieth Century Norfolk* and co-author of *Blacks in the Industrial Age: A Documentary History.*